The Films of
Roger Corman

'Shooting My Way Out of Trouble'

ALAN FRANK

BT Batsford Ltd · London

Printed by The Bath Press, Bath

for the publishers
BT Batsford
583 Fulham Road
London
SW6 5BY

ISBN 0 7134 8272 9

A catalogue record for this book is available from the British Library

Illustrations courtesy of the British Film Institute and Gary Parfitt

CONTENTS

Introduction

If it wasn't for Roger Corman, I would now be a doctor, not a writer.

Actually, that is not entirely fair – there are other, less interesting filmmakers who must share some of the blame – but the truth is that when I look back to my days as a medical student at Cambridge, I have to admit that I spent rather more time watching movies than dissecting bodies. Result – I gave up medicine (due to injury sustained in an unfortunate laboratory accident, and not as would have been true justice, the result of sloth compounded with cinema-going).

My addictive attachment to the cinema was looked upon as deeply unfortunate by my tutors who had every reason to disapprove. My friends were not impressed either since at the time movies had not the intellectual cachet they possess today and they wrongly believed I was wasting my time and money.

Then I had no intellectual approach to the cinema but simply savoured the pleasure of getting two films for the price of one and if any of them carried a subtext I don't suppose that I noticed or cared about depth or lack of it. I had grown up in east Africa where double bills did not exist and so it wasn't until I came to Britain that I saw a B feature. In fact, it took me a while to discover the difference between A films and the cheaper, shorter movies that made up double bills. Finally, I figured out that thrillers with faded Hollywood stars whom I thought were dead helping Scotland Yard solve cheap crimes or working for British newspapers and low-budget American pictures of almost every genre were actually not the movies people paid to see. They merely came with the package.

By then, though, it was too late for me to reform. I was hooked on the gutsier, more vivid and more thoroughly entertaining American B features, preferring them to their more decorous, less emotive British counterparts.

This was the heyday of Roger Corman, years before his long overdue canonization by the slow-on-the-uptake opinion-makers of journals like *Monthly Film Bulletin*. I would seek out his movies when they joined their allegedly more prestigious partners at the bottom of double bills. I had never ever heard of *auterism*, but I knew what I liked and what I liked was Corman.

I still do and I hope this book reflects my admiration and respect for him and for the sheer enjoyment his movies have given and continue to give me.

Alan Frank
London 1998

Dedication
This is for (alphabetically) Ben (*Teenage Caveman)*, Kate (*The Raven*), and Liza (*The Undead*) and, of course, for Gilly (*Voyage to the Planet of Prehistoric Women*)

Acknowledgements
My sincere thanks to Gerald Aaron (who helps keep me solvent), Ann Billson, Vikki Cook, Nathalie Dejonghe, Dave Fuller, Kim Newman, Gary Parfitt, Laszlo Svaty Pramen, David Quinlan, Carol Reyes, William D Russell, Susan Sackier, Warren Sherman, Christopher Tookey, Bill Winborn, to everyone at the BFI National Library for their invaluable help and unfailing courtesy and, especially, to Roger Corman for making time in his busy schedule to talk to me in Los Angeles.

Part 1

Some Facts in the Case of Mr Roger Corman

This book is about the *films* of Roger Corman. It is not intended to be a biography since, apart from any other considerations, Corman has already written his hugely entertaining *How I Made a Hundred Movies in Hollywood and Never Lost a Dime*. Nevertheless, there are some basic biographical details which are well worth noting. Roger William Corman was born in Detroit on 5 April, 1926, sharing the date, if not the year, with, among others, Bette Davis, Spencer Tracy, Melvyn Douglas and, appropriately, Gregory Peck who in 1951 starred in *The Gunfighter*, the first film to be produced from a screenplay on which Corman had worked.

When his engineer father retired, the family moved from Detroit to Los Angeles. Corman attended Beverly Hills High School where, almost inevitably given the milieu and the Hollywood-oriented alumni, he became fascinated with the cinema. He read omnivorously, including the works of Edgar Allan Poe which were to serve as the basis for his seminal series of Sixties horror movies.

His pre-college studies focused on mathematics, physics and chemistry since at that time he intended to become an engineer like his father. So, after graduating from High School in 1943, he went on to read engineering at Stanford University.

'I think I probably chose the wrong major in university', he said. 'I probably shouldn't have been an engineering major, but my father had been an engineer and I followed in his footsteps. I probably should have been an English literature major, because from early youth I read novels, short stories – anything I could get my hands on – and I think as such that helped me; it gave me a valuable background in literature. Engineering

gave me a certain training, a certain educational background and prepared me; but I think anybody who works in a creative way is working partially out of their conscious mind and partially out of their unconscious mind, so much of what I did and the way I did it I would have probably done whether I had probably studied engineering or not. Engineering gave me a little additional knowledge, although a lot of it was, as you say, flying by the seat of my pants.'

While at Stanford, Corman turned to freelance writing and sold articles to *Popular Mechanics* and *Science and Mechanics* before volunteering for officer training in the World War Two US Navy. He served three years in the Navy and then went back to Stanford for his senior year under the GI Bill. He graduated in 1947 with a degree in Industrial Engineering and then returned to Los Angeles.

However, engineering no longer represented a career goal and, fired by his passion for films and further writing experience at university, Corman decided to break into movies. He did, initially as a messenger boy at 20th Century-Fox where he rose to become a story analyst before he left to spend a sabbatical in Europe, including a term as a postgraduate student reading English literature at Oxford University.

He returned to Hollywood where – after a stint as a literary agent – he went on to become, in the words of British critic Peter John Dyer, 'The Orson Welles of Z movies'. He directed 28 films during his B feature heyday from 1954 and 1960 before embarking on the bigger-budgeted Edgar Allan Poe cycle of Gothic shockers that brought him mainstream critical approval and cult status (long after moviegoers had learned to appreciate

him) with *The Fall of the House of Usher*.

In the Sixties his output was less prolific and he directed only 20 films between 1960 and 1970. However, this period saw him becoming an increasingly busy independent producer. In that capacity and especially after he formed his own New World Pictures, Corman played midwife to some of Hollywood's major talents-to-be including Francis Ford Coppola, Martin Scorsese, Jonathan Demme, Gale Ann Hurd, James Cameron, Gary Kurtz and Joe Dante who had once reviewed Corman's pictures in the fanzine *Castle of Frankenstein*.

Says Corman: 'It started with Francis Coppola, Peter Bogdanovich and a number of others who came out of my staff to direct. But at the beginning I was just looking for good members of the crew.'

Corman spoke of some of his other 'graduates'.

'Jonathan Demme has succeeded. Alan Arkush isn't as well known as some of the others, but he is a very well-regarded television director who primarily does pilots, which is an extremely well-paid job because under the Directors Guild rules, if you direct the pilot for a series you get a royalty from every single episode. So Alan specializes in this.

'Jim Cameron has gotten bigger and bigger and bigger. When I was talking to Cameron and Gale Hurd after *The Terminator* and they told me, "We did the things that we did when we were with you but we had more money and we did them bigger." They continued when they were together very effectively and Gale has continued following that line, maybe a little bit more than Jim has. Jim has gotten bigger, but I will say this for Jim, I don't believe he deliberately wastes money. I think he honestly believes that he is making the best possible picture of the kind of picture he wants to make.'

Corman was right as usual and the Oscar-garlanded success of Cameron's *Titanic* against the commercial odds proves his point.

'I believe you have to gamble, you have to take chances. You can't just keep turning out the same thing.'

After making *Von Richthofen and Brown*, Corman quit direction. 'I just got tired. Every day I would drive out from Dublin to the airport which was out location and there was a fork in the road – one way to this airport and the other to Galway Bay – and every morning I was tempted to swing the car in the other direction and go to Galway Bay and just sit and look at the ocean. But every morning I went dutifully to the airport and did my work. But I knew that I had to stop.

'What I planned to do was simply to take the traditional sabbatical. I decided I would stop for one year and then start directing again. But during that year I thought it would be interesting to start a little production and distribution company, which was New World, and it got off to an incredible start. Our first picture was a big success; our second was a big success; by the end of the year we were a fairly important company. I couldn't find anyone else to run it, so I just stayed on and I kept thinking, well, in another year or so I will go back to directing – and I never really did.'

Corman formed New World Pictures in 1970. 'I felt that if I were going to produce as many films as I intended to I had to have my own distribution,' he said. 'I could not be dependent on somebody else for distribution. It's partially that distributors never tell you the truth, but also they're not efficient on your behalf. If you're the outside producer say, for a company like American International or Allied Artists, their in-house productions are going to get better distribution. You're going to be treated all right but not with the same intensity.'

The industry was surprised. 'Some people said – in a friendly way – that I was clearly a schizophrenic. I even said it myself. But I always loved the works of Fellini, Bergman, Kurosawa. I had felt that their films were not distributed as well as they should have been. They were either being distributed by small companies who were really sort of aficionados rather than efficient distribution companies, or they were being distributed by the majors who are excellent but aren't really geared to that type of film, and possibly don't understand exactly how to distribute that type of film.

'We started in 1970 and within 18 months we were the strongest independent distribution company in the country. I think we passed American International very quickly.

'New World was becoming identified with the type of films we were making, which was frankly American low-budget commercial films, and I wanted to expand the name to more prestigious films.

'What I *really* wanted to do was to distribute these films, and see that they got a good audience. I did not want to lose money but I did not anticipate or, I should

say, I did not *expect* to make a great deal of money. I felt that if I could break even or make a little money, that would be fine. It was what I wanted to do and that's exactly what happened. I made a little bit of money overall and on couple of them I made a lot of money, on a couple of them I didn't, but in summing it all up commercially, it was slightly profitable. I would say this – it was a satisfactorily profitable operation and it was pleasing to me to have done it.

What are you doing putting a Bergman film into a drive-in?

'We made a point of opening, as you always do, at the art houses of New York and Los Angeles and so forth, but then moving into the commercial houses and occasionally into the drive-ins. I put one of Bergman's films – I think it was *Cries and Whispers* –into a drive-in in Louisiana and I got a letter saying, "What are you doing putting a Bergman film into a drive-in?" What happened was that I put it in at the end of the drive-in season when the drive-ins didn't have an adequate supply of the type of film they normally used, but there was still some business to be done. And frankly, the owners didn't particularly care what they were screening and so they took it because they had taken other films from New World. And they did average business. They were delighted to have a picture that would do average business and for a Bergman film to do average business in a drive-in was wonderful for everybody.

'Bergman wrote me a letter, a kind of a funny letter thanking me, saying he had never anticipated reaching that audience but he was delighted to have a different audience see his films. Any filmmaker wants to have his films seen.

'I was attempting to build New World as – not a major, we used the word *boutique* and I think it is still being used correctly for companies like Miramax and New Line, the founders of which have both told me they founded their companies after New World. I wanted to distribute *all* types of films, I wanted to distribute commercial films, art films and films that had some aspects of both.'

In 1983, Corman sold New World for $17 million and then went straight back into business again as a producer-distributor, first as Millennium (1983) then New Horizons (1984) and Concorde (1985).

Ten years later, under the headline 'Thrifty Corman

healthy in 4th Decade', *Variety* noted 'the silver-haired but forever-young chief of Concorde-New Horizons Pictures keeps his feet on the ground and money in the till making cheap genre movies, a career that began in 1954 with his $12,000 *Monster From the Ocean Floor*. He has since produced more than 250 films.'

By 1995, however, the nature of the business had changed radically and home video and television had replaced cinemas as the major mediums for movies.

'It's unfortunate. When I started, every film played in theatres. Now I would say three-quarters or even 80 percent – I would say 80 percent of our films – don't even appear in theatres in the United States. They either go straight to home video or to Cable TV.

'We have got a deal for the last three years with Showtime, the cable network, for a series called *Roger Corman Presents*. These are a variation on the 1950s exploitation Bs, but those actually didn't do that well and I think Showtime never understood why. They have had good reviews and a lot of publicity but the ratings were not quite as high as they wanted. I believe the reason was that Showtime and the people who made them thought of them as camp and made them that way. When they were originally made, nobody thought of them as camp. We were trying to make good, low budget films.

'So when they asked me to do this series they were still thinking vaguely camp and I figured there is no reason for me to get into any heavy discussions with them. I know they're going to be science fiction and horror films.

'They wanted to remake a few of my old ones and the rest would be originals. And I said it's the same as it used to be. We are simply going to do the best science fiction and horror films under the given circumstances. There is no attempt to make them as camp films and as a result they have been the highest rated shows they have had.

We deliberately try, as it were, to push the envelope. We try to go as far as we can in each film. For instance, I have a problem with Showtime right now on a picture we are tentatively calling *Club Vampire* which is shot and written and directed by Andy Rubin who is a first-time director. He shot it in an almost surreal fashion which I like very much, but which Showtime hates. They have difficulty following what's going on and we are doing some work in post-production to clarify it. I wouldn't

say that Showtime is completely wrong. It was a little bit maybe indecipherable in the first cut but it will end up very much as a surreal picture. But we think it will be clear enough that you can follow it – and Showtime will hate it right to the end. I know that. It's their own feeling. I think most of these large organisations end up with self-imposed rules. They don't want to gamble.'

Corman continues to specialize in producing fast-moving audience-friendly genre pictures that are, in essence, B movies with A-list casts and usually larger – for him – budgets ranging from low ($1 million) to medium ($2 million) to large ($4 million). He also still continues to operate the kind of ingenious economies in production that he pioneered in the Sixties when he bought the 1960 Russian science fiction movie *Nebo Zovet* and reused its special effects as stock footage to improve films like *Battle Beyond the Sun*. Now he reuses footage from his older movies to enhance new productions.

'It's not paying homage,' he explained. 'We do it simply to make a low budget picture look bigger. We use it probably more in science fiction pictures than in any other, because we spent, particularly in *Battle Beyond the Stars* and in *Galaxy of Terror*, we spent quite a bit of money for us on the spaceships, both of them. The spaceships were done by Jim Cameron and they looked very good so we'd use those over and over. We have done new work but I would say a lot of the new work is not as good as what Jim did 20 years ago.

'I don't put my name on all the films, but I have produced or co-produced over 400. My style is this. I work with the writer and with the director in preproduction. During production I make a point of either never going to the set or going to the set only once or twice, just to have coffee and say 'hello' because I found early on that people would turn to me and ask me questions when they should have been asking the same questions of the director. So I thought it's better for me not to be here, and I would look at the dailies – although I don't look at the dailies any more.

'If I had something to say to the director, I would call him in the evening or at the lunch hour so that I wouldn't be seen on the set talking to the director. Then I always give the director two cuts. I never look at the first or second cut... I will then come in on the second cut with members of my staff and we will look at each cut, give our notes to the director and the editor with the proviso, oh, I shouldn't say the 'proviso', with the statement they are not obligated to follow all of the notes, they are obligated to *consider* the notes but the notes they disagree with to ignore. That's generally the way we function.'

Corman decides on the year's slate of films
'Now, during the year, the plan will change. But at the beginning of the year I will have a very well-formed schedule for the first six months of the year – well, loosely – and a loose schedule for the second six months, knowing that I will probably be changing that second six months a fair amount as we get into the year and one script doesn't turn out as well as I thought. Or maybe I get a new idea and I say, let's do this and get a script quickly or something like that.

'It is very convenient for critics to say that the director does everything. Having been a director, a producer and a writer, I believe it's a three-way street; that everybody contributes *in general*, the director contributes a little bit more than the producer and the writer, but not always.

'It is still fun,' he added. 'But it's not quite as much fun as it used to be. I have been doing it a long time now, over 40 years, and I try to be as innovative as I can. But making 20 to 30 pictures a year, which is what I do, inevitably there is a certain repetition to it. So that bothers me a little bit.

'And unfortunately I find myself becoming more and more involved with the *business* and less and less involved with the creative side, and that bothers me. I'm trying to delegate more of the business end and get back heavily into the creative side of it. I still enjoy it, but I have to admit I don't enjoy it quite as much as I did as a young man. Maybe you could say the same thing about sex: it changes a little bit when you get older.'

When I asked him how he would best like to be remembered – as a writer, a director or as a producer, he told me: 'I would say that I would like to be remembered as a filmmaker, that I simply have made motion pictures.'

His former protégé Martin Scorsese put it perfectly when he said: 'Roger Corman is not only a great mentor. He's an artist, the best kind of artist, able to nurture and inspire talent in a generous way.'

And, perhaps more than any other filmaker before or since, Corman has always been a master of the enviable art of shooting his way out of trouble.

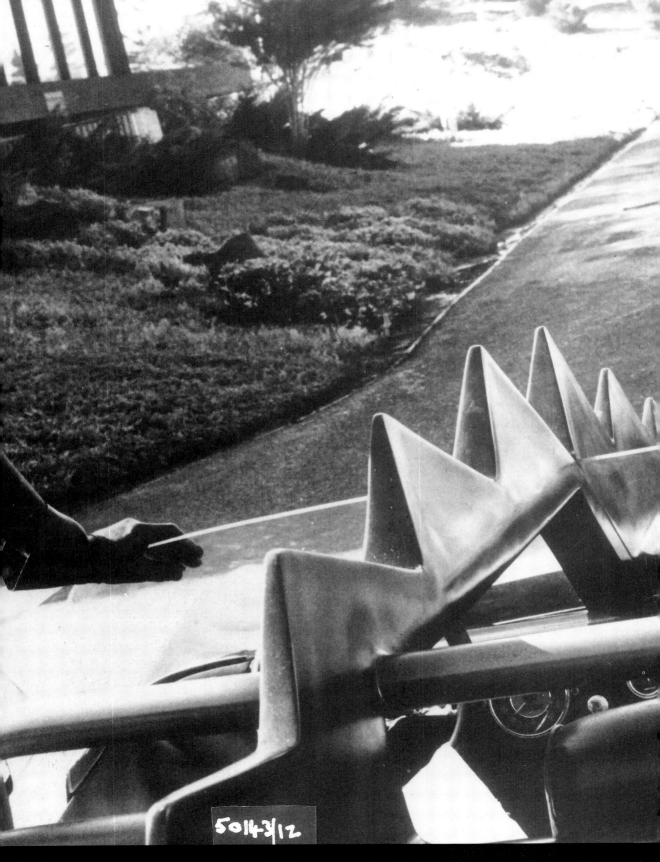

5014 3/12

Death Race 2000

Part 2

KING OF THE Bs

The greatest independent filmmaker the American industry has ever seen and will probably ever see... a wildly gifted, masterful director when he chooses to be.

Jonathan Demme

Corman gained his first toehold in films in 1948 when the father of a friend fixed up a job for him as a messenger at 20th Century-Fox for $32.50 a week where he worked on Saturdays for no pay so that he could spend time watching movies being made. He also read scripts over weekends for the story department.

His persistence paid off and in 1949 he was appointed as a story analyst at $65 a week. Most of his work involved reading and analyzing minor screenplays that had been sent in on spec by agents. However, he did play midwife to *The Gunfighter* when he worked up a screenplay called *The Big Gun* and passed it on to a senior studio producer: it was eventually filmed (as *The Gunfighter*) with Gregory Peck.

'I think I probably chose the wrong major in university. I probably shouldn't have been an engineering major, but my father had been an engineer and I followed in his footsteps. I probably should have been an English literature major, because from early youth I read novels, short stories, anything I could get my hands on

and I think as such that helped me; it simply gave me a background in literature.'

Corman decided he wanted to write his own screenplays and thought experience of life in Europe would be an advantage. After reading Modern English Literature for a term as a postgraduate student at Oxford University under the GI Bill, he spent time in Paris.

Then, at the end of his year-long European 'sabbatical', he returned to Los Angeles where he got a job with the Jules Goldstone literary agency, segued from there to work briefly as a grip for KLAC TV and then returned to reading scripts for the Dick Highland Agency. He sold his first screenplay (co-written with a friend, U S Anderson) for $3,000 to Allied Artists, who changed the title from *The House in the Sea* to *Highway Dragnet* to cash in on the then popular Jack Webb television show. When he saw the finished film, Corman was appalled at the damage done to his screenplay during production and decided he could do better. His initiation on *Highway Dragnet* was not a total letdown, however, since it earned him the Associate Producer credit that helped him get his first production, *It Stalked the Ocean Floor/The Monster From the Ocean Floor,* off the sea bed.

THE MONSTER FROM THE OCEAN FLOOR

'Shoestringer which has story value.'

Backstory

Having read an article in the *Los Angeles Times* about a new electric-powered, one-man submarine, Corman contacted the makers, Aerojet General, and parleyed himself the free use of a submarine in exchange for publicity and an on-screen credit.

Corman wrote the original story and hired writer William Danch to write the screenplay. Corman had some $3,500 of his own and, after his parents turned down his request for backing, raised cash selling shares to friends, finally going into production when Consolidated Laboratories agreed to process the film for a deferred $5,000.

'From the beginning I worked with union crews. The first picture I ever produced was *It Stalked the Ocean Floor* which the distributor changed to *Monster from the Ocean Floor* because he thought *It Stalked the Ocean Floor* was too arty. I had Wyott Ordung as director and he shot the picture in six days for, I think, $12,000 cash and some deferments which I think brought it up close to $30,000.'

It was shot rapidly on location around Malibu (setting the pattern for his fast, no-frills style of filmmaking) with Corman doubling as grip and driver as well as producer.

Jonathan Haze made his film debut, going on to become a member of Corman's low-budget repertory company. While working at the Tide Oil Company gas station on Santa Monica Boulevard, Haze had met Ordung who told him, 'Wow, you're a great type! One of these days I'm going to make a movie and I'm gonna put you in it!'. 'And', said Haze, 'I'd say, "Oh yeah, great". Then one night he came in and said, "I just made a movie deal with a guy named Roger Corman and I'm going to direct it! It's called *The Monster from the Ocean Floor* and there's a part in it of a Mexican deep-sea diver that you'd be great for! Would you grow a moustache?" So I did *Monster* and Roger and I got to be friends.'

Story

An American artist working in Mexico convinces a marine biologist of the existence of a sea monster which he kills by ramming the creature in its single eye with his one-man submarine.

Corman's first production suffers from slow direction, too much tedious dialogue and insufficient action: the film is dull and the monster (built by puppeteer Bob Baker) looks (and was) cheap – but the film made money.

Reviews

'Here's an oddity – a well-done quickie. Lensed entirely along the coast of lower California, *Monster from the Ocean Floor* boasts an interest-holding story, good direction and performances, with an added plus factor being a tag that's fully exploitable... Roger Corman's production supervision has packed the footage with commercial values without going overboard, while Wyott Ordung's surprisingly good direction has drawn all the suspense from the William Danch screenplay.'
Variety

'Second feature for the unsophisticated... the monster appears only in a few scenes towards the end and is poorly presented. This film includes a number of under-

water scenes which are adequately done, but there is little excitement, the story is weak and the acting is
wooden.'
CEA Film Report

'Not even the most gluttonous science fiction addicts
are likely to derive enjoyment from this picture, with its
indifferent trick work, unlikely monster and threadbare
plot.'
Monthly Film Bulletin

CREDITS

The Monster From The Ocean Floor (1954)
pc Palo Alto.   **p** Roger Corman.
d Wyott Ordung.   **w** William Danch.
ph Floyd Crosby.   **bw. ed** Ed Samson.
ad Ben Hayne.   **m** André Brumer.
64 mins.
Cast: Anne Kimbell (Julie Blair), Stuart Wade (Steve Dunning),
Dick Pinner (Dr Baldwin), Jack Hayes (Jonathan Haze) (Joe),
Wyott Ordung (Pablo), Inez Palange (Tula)

THE FAST AND THE FURIOUS

> **'Chase meller with sports car racing theme; for lowercase programmer dates.'**

I think he gave a lot of people opportunities to do things they would've never gotten otherwise. I personally owe a lot to Roger. He gave me a career as an actor.
Jonathan Haze

Corman's brother Gene arranged distribution of *The Monster from the Ocean Floor* with Robert Lippert who also provided an advance of $60,000, which enabled Corman to pay the negative costs on the picture, repay the money he had borrowed and to begin production on *The Fast and the Furious.*

Backstory

Even with a considerably larger ($50,000) budget than *The Monster from the Ocean Floor*, Corman needed known actors for less than their usual fees: he persuaded John Ireland to appear by letting him direct (in tandem with editor Edward Samson). Said Ireland: 'I'd never directed a film before. I enjoyed the hustle and spontaneity of it.' There certainly must have been quite a hustle since the film was shot in just nine days.

The budget was further maximised when Corman obtained Jaguar racing cars in exchange for free product placement. He filmed the racing footage during the Jaguar Open Sports Car race at Monterey: other sequences were shot at Port Dume and, again, around Malibu. Corman went behind one of two cameras used to cover the race and, as a result, decided that directing was his real metier.

Not being able to afford two stunt drivers, he also took the wheel as Ireland's opponent and, unfortunately, won the race, which then had to be re-staged: 'I got so excited about driving a real race car that I drove to win the race. I wouldn't admit that to anybody at the time,

but I wasn't about to come in second just because the script said so.'

Corman received distribution offers from Columbia, Republic and Allied Artists but wanted to use *The Fast and the Furious* as his calling card to negotiate a multi-picture deal. James H Nicholson, who had been sales manager of Realart, and lawyer Samuel Z Arkoff were in the process of forming their own distribution company, American Releasing Corporation, which went on to become American International Pictures, the biggest and most profitable independent production and distribution outfit in the 1950s and 1960s. They agreed to a three-picture deal, with *The Fast and the Furious* as the first film.

'Of course, Jim and I realised that *The Fast and the Furious* was no *Gone With the Wind*. But not too many pictures are. Both Ireland and Malone had some name value, and we concluded that the movie had enough positive elements that we might be able to make some money with it. We needed a picture, and we had finally found one,' said Arkoff. It was the start of a long and mutually profitable collaboration that lasted until *Gas-s-s-s!* in 1970.

Story

A trucker who has been falsely jailed for murder breaks out of jail and goes on the run, commandeering the car of a female driver competing in an automobile race that will take him across the Mexican border.

Serviceable melodrama whose rousing four-wheeled action impresses rather more than its acting.

Reviews

'Chase meller with sports car racing theme; for lowercase programmer dates. High-priced sportscar bombs

furnish most of the action for *The Fast and the Furious*, a modestly budgeted chase meller that is slanted for lowercase programmer bookings. Racing footage is interesting but becomes repetitious and helps string out the running time to an unnecessary 73 minutes, an unhandy length for supporting play dates. New indie distribution outfit, American Releasing Corp. is handling the Palo Alto production as the first of four features from the latter unit... Producer Roger Corman furnished the story.'
Variety

'... a second feature for the masses... This is a heavy picture and the leading character is by no means a pleasant personality and little sympathy for him is aroused. Most of the action consists of motor journeys and en route there is much quarrelling and bickering. The acting is satisfactory, but the players have little real opportunity. The film is a modest second feature.'
CEA Film Report

'After a promising start, the film quickly fades; dialogue is artificial and inept, the playing of John Ireland and Dorothy Malone barely manages to hold an indifferently constructed story together, and we are left with a few motor racing sequences which might have made the film worthwhile had they been rather more fast or furious.'
Monthly Film Bulletin

CREDITS ▷▷▷▷▷▷▷▷▷▷▷▷

The Fast And The Furious (1954)
pc Palo Alto   **p, st** Roger Corman
d Edward Samson, John Ireland   **w** Jerome Odlum, Jean Howell
ph Floyd Crosby   **bw.**
ed Edward Samson   **m** Alexander Gerens
65 mins
Cast: John Ireland (Frank Webster), Dorothy Malone (Connie Adair), Bruce Carlisle (Faber), Marshall Bradford (Race official), Jean Howell (Sally), Larry Thor (Police Sergeant), Robin Morse (Gas Station Attendant), Bruno DeSota (Truck Driver), Iris Adrian (Waitress)

FIVE GUNS WEST

'Acceptable fare for the smaller outdoor situations.'

Roger is a unique man who marches to a different drummer.
Sam Arkoff

'Jim and I had a relationship with Roger that we've never had with anyone else', said Arkoff. 'We shook hands when we made a deal and sometimes never had a written contract until after the picture was finished. Roger always delivered his films and we always paid him promptly.' Corman made his directorial debut with his second film for Arkoff and Nicholson, *Five Guns West*.

Backstory

Corman had come to realise that the most effective way to keep control of his films was to double as producer and director. He engaged R Wright Campbell as screenwriter for $200 and then gave him a role when Campbell pointed out that the Screen Actors Guild membership meant even the bit-part actors were being paid more than he was. Before Corman embarked on direction, he decided to have a dry run by directing an eight-minute short, written by a friend and using his key grip Chuck Hannawalt's 16mm camera and lighting equipment, but he never got around to editing the footage. Instead (after throwing up from nerves while driving to the location on the first day) he took a crash course in practical filmmaking while shooting *Five Guns West*, largely on location, driving himself, his actors and crew through gruelling ten-hour days and establishing an excellent rapport with cinematographer (and frequent future collaborator) Floyd Crosby and art

director/Western buff Ben Haye.

He also stayed in character and stretched his budget by using bought-in stock Indian footage to beef up the action sequences.

Said Mike Connors, 'Roger was one of the few people around who gave inexperienced actors a chance. I got, I think, $400. But just working was a great thrill. Roger had real nervous energy and a very analytical mind. He didn't waste time going for extra coverage or needless takes. Even then, he was a great razzle-dazzle man in getting the most on the screen for the least amount.'

Story

Five killers due to be hanged are pardoned providing they join the Confederate Army towards the end of the Civil War and, led by Sturges, are sent to hold up a Union stagecoach carrying a shipment of gold and a Southern traitor.

Corman's first film as director is a competent, unpretentious but otherwise unremarkable second feature Western that stretches its patently low budget efficiently.

Reviews

'Acceptable fare for the smaller outdoor situations. The entertainment values aren't all they should be for the action trade, but the pic should prove out for releases intentions as a bill-filler... Campbell's plotting is acceptable but he permits his characters to talk too much. The result is that the pacing by producer Roger Corman, on his first directorial assignment, lags often enough to

make the unspooling seem slow. Too, Corman doesn't supply as much drive to the action as this type of subject requires so the elements of suspense and tension present in the story aren't fully realised.'
Variety

'This is a Western with a good quota of action, a well-developed and not too stereotyped story, a romantic interest and a fast-moving climax.'
CEA Film Report

'A capable lower-bracket Western. Characterisations are firmer and more individual than in many films of this type, and the script is competently done with an occa-sional suggestion of originality.'
Monthly Film Bulletin

CREDITS

Five Guns West (US 1954)
pc American Releasing Corporation/Palo Alto
p, d, st Roger Corman   **w** R Wright Campbell
ph Floyd Crosby   colour.
ed Ronald Sinclair   **ad** Ben Hayne
m Buddy Bregman   78 mins.
Cast: John Lund (Govern Sturges), Dorothy Malone (Shaleee), Touch Connors (Hale Clinton), Bob Campbell (John Candy), Jonathan Haze (Billy Candy) Paul Birch (J C Haggard), James Stone (Uncle Mime), Jack Ingraham (Jethro), Larry Thor (Confederate Captain)

AIP provided the title, and Corman filmed *The Oklahoma Woman* for some $60,000 in black and white and Superscope: as with his three other Westerns of the period, Corman gave atypical prominence to his leading ladies.

'The one thing that can be said for working with him is that Roger didn't spend a lot of time romancing anybody, or with nonsense. Roger would say, "Here on page 20, I'd like to have some violence." You'd say, "Roger, there's no motivation for it."
'"Well", Roger would say, "find a reason for it because it seems to me that it's slowing down and the crowd that comes to out pictures wants to see a little something".'
R Wright Campbell

Backstory
Executive producer Alex Gordon was left to arbitrate after Corman signed Castle to play Denning's former lover: she wanted top billing (after Denning) while Downs expected the same. Eventually a deal was struck which gave Castle top billing but in the same type size as Downs, who would be starred in another AIP movie.

Story
A former gunslinger is released from prison but when he goes home to claim the ranch he has inherited his one-time girlfriend sets out to frame him for murder.

The action is vigorous, Castle and Downs are surprisingly feminist protagonists for the period but inferior

THE DAY THE WORLD ENDED

The success of his first foray into science fiction – the most popular of all his B film genres – with *The Day the World Ended* confirmed his accomplishment as a director and proved his considerable value to AIP. This was the first of the five films Beverly Garland made for Corman.

Backstory

'It was really amazing to see how smoothly Roger handled everything,' said producer Alex Gordon of Corman's first science fiction/horror movie which was blessed with a title dreamed up by AIP's Jim Nicholson, a low ($96,000) budget and a brief shooting schedule – seven days on location in Bronson Canyon near Los Angeles' Griffith Park and a further three days at the Sportsman's Lodge Restaurant.

Released as the top half of a double feature with *The Phantom From 10,000 Leagues*, it was a commercial success and established him as a genre director. The mutant, created and performed by Paul Blaisdell who dubbed it 'Marty', was built from foam rubber. It featured claws from a magic shop, finger and toenails carved from white pine and its teeth compiled from commercially available fangs.

Blaisdell was not very tall (5' 7") and had to peer through the mutant's mouth to get his bearings which caused problems when he came to carry off Lori Nelson. He also almost drowned when 'Marty' died and the monster suit filled up with water.

Clearly an actor manqué, Blaisdell was quoted as saying 'I've often wondered why the guy who plays the monster in a monster movie is invariably listed last in the credits.'

Story

Seven disparate survivors of a 1970 nuclear holocaust (Total Destruction Day) hole up together in an uneasy alliance in a mountain house and are menaced by mutants.

Appropriately for the period, the real 'monster' is The Bomb. Corman deepens the drama by balancing the box-office appeal of the science fiction-horror elements with a moderately tense, if schematic, study of people under stress: the three-horned mutant may be unlikely but it is certainly memorable.

Reviews

'Packs enough novelty in its plot theme to carry off its horror chores satisfactorily, even though imagination runs away with the subject at times and the dialogue is inclined to be static and direction slow-paced ... no great demands are made by script and direction.'
Variety

'There are some rather gruesome shots, the subject is naively handled, the story is only mildly exciting and on the slow side, the dialogue is trite and the acting is barely adequate. The picture makes only moderate entertainment for uncritical devotees of science fiction.'
CEA Film Report

'Further evidence of the deterioration of standards in science fiction. The monster, although more flamboyantly decorated that most of his recent colleagues, is no less ludicrous. The film is in all respects naïve and artless.'
Monthly Film Bulletin

'Fast direction by Roger Corman.'
Castle of Frankenstein

'Hearty congratulations to the players, for they manage to keep their faces straight throughout the film.'
Picturegoer

CREDITS

The Day the World Ended (US 1955)
pc American Releasing Corporation/Golden State
exec p Alex Gordon   **p, d** Roger Corman
w Lou Russoff   **ph** Jock Feindel
bw.   **ed** Ronald Sinclair
sfx/mutant design Paul Blaisdell **m** Ronald Stein
79 mins.
Cast: Richard Denning (Rick), Lori Nelson (Louise Maddison), Adele Jergens (Runy), Touch (later Mike) Connors (Tony), Paul Birch (Maddison), Raymond Hatton (Pete), Paul Dubov (Radek), Jonathan Haze (Contaminated man), Paul Blaisdell (Mutant)

For his fourth and final B feature Western Corman asked Charles Griffith to switch the standard genre plot by having the sheriff die in the course of his duty and his widow strap on six-guns and clean up the town as firmly as any man.

Backstory

Corman, never one to miss an opportunity, seized the day and embarked on one final six-day Western before the five-day week negotiated by the studios with the IATSE became mandatory. Unfortunately, it rained for five days, turning the locations to mud and miring trucks and equipment. As a result *Gunslinger* took seven days to shoot and became his only film (co-financed with his brother Gene) to go over schedule.

Allison Hayes suffered the appalling conditions along with the rest of the cast and crew, but didn't remain silent, asking instead: 'Tell me, Roger. Who do I have to fuck to get *off* this picture?' In the event, however, she exited after she broke her arm falling off her horse. Corman took the opportunity while waiting for transport to take her to hospital to shoot (with Hayes' approval) a reel of close-ups.

Beverley Garland, too, had her share of misfortune. She sprained her ankle running down the saloon stairs but continued to work after her ankle was anaesthetized with novocaine; and she and Ireland were bitten by ants while playing a romantic scene.

Story

A gunslinger is hired by a crooked female saloon owner to kill the woman who takes over as Marshal when her husband is killed, but he falls for his intended victim.

Standard B feature Western fare which rarely rises above its shoestring budget but the pace is brisk, there

Gunslinger
1956 Corman's only film to go over schedule

are a few interesting plot twists and the muddy settings, while not planned, sometimes add surreal touches to the proceedings.

Reviews

'The Roger Corman production should get its share of playing time attention in the programme market... the script and Corman's direction lean heavily on sex, sometimes justifiably in view of the story twist, and sometimes ludicrously... Corman unwisely tries to dress up values with a chorus line in Miss Hayes' saloon, but since there are only three femmes doing poor routines it adds up to nothing.'
Variety

'This is a leisurely moving and not entirely convincing story, but it has a rather unusual twist in that it concerns a woman sheriff and has a fair share of action, some of which is rather violent. It makes quite good supporting entertainment for devotees of tough Westerns.'
CEA Film Report

'A routine, often violent Western which manages to sustain the interest due to some restrained playing and well-presented backgrounds. The climax is slightly unusual in that the female Marshal finally overcomes her emotions and despatches her outlaw lover.'
Monthly Film Bulletin

CREDITS

Gunslinger (US 1956)
pc American Releasing Corporation/Roger Corman Production
p, d Roger Corman   **w** Charles B Griffith, Mark Hanna
ph Fred West   colour
ed Charles Gross   **m** Ronald Stein
77 mins.
Cast: John Ireland (Cane Miro), Beverly Garland (Rose Hood), Allison Hayes (Erica Page), Martin Kingsley (Gideon Polk), Jonathan Haze (Jack Hays), Chris Alcaide (Joshua Tate), Richard Miller (Jimmy Tonto), Bruno Ve Sota (Zebelon Tabb), Margaret Campbell (Felicity Polk), William Schallert (Scott Hood), Aaron Saxon (Nate Signo), Chris Miller (Tessie-Belle)

SWAMP WOMEN

'Weak filler fare with exploitable title.'

Corman took his cast and crew to Louisiana to make *Swamp Women* for the Woolner Brothers who owned a circuit of drive-in cinemas in New Orleans. Five of his films would be released in 1956. He would be even more prolific the following year which saw nine Corman pictures make their way into cinemas.

Roger said to me, 'You're really one of the best stuntwomen I have ever worked with'.
Beverly Garland

Backstory

Once again the actors suffered for their art. Garland recalled, 'I can remember being up this tree, and there was a snake, and then somebody shoots me. The stunt man told me he'd be there to catch me. And boy, I made a fall that, if he hadn't been there, I would have killed myself. In those days you did all your own stunts, all your own everything. We walked through the swamp and it was just unbelievable, but we did it. Through the muck and the mire, but it was fun, interesting. We were all young and we loved it.'

Story

Three escaped female convicts and an undercover policewoman seeking stolen diamonds hidden in the swamps of Louisiana steal a boat from a geologist, leaving his girlfriend to be eaten by alligators who claim another victim before justice finally prevails.

The Louisiana bayou backgrounds are the most convincing aspect of a luridly enjoyable prison-break melodrama whose ten-day shoot hardly shook the world.

Reviews

'**Weak filler fare with exploitable title**. Only meagre entertainment is dished out in *Swamp Women* ... pic's chief asset is its exploitable tag; otherwise, it's just filler material ... Roger Corman's direction, somewhat over-melodramatic, fully utilizes the bayou area to pictorial advantage, with Fred West's Eastman Color camara work also aiding here.'
Variety

'Popular appeal is here in the form of melodrama, sex and female gangsterism, while tough femininity slogging it out in the Louisiana swamps is the theme of the somewhat squalid and certainly unrealistic tale ... perhaps the most convincing thing in the entire film is the natural backgrounds of the swamps ... the action is mainly of the fistic bashing and hair-tearing order, thanks to the readiness of one of the girls to do battle, but there is also some desultory gunplay and spearwork towards the end. In addition to its narrative crudity, the tale is not markedly eventful, while the interpolated Mardi Gras scenes, though adding some pictorial interest, are not of the highest quality. Only uncritical filmgoers are likely to regard the concoctions with pleasurable interest, but for such tastes the abundance of surface action might well be sufficient to save the entertainment day.'
CEA Film Report

'This feminine version of the conventional escape story, with its search for hidden treasure, is given a new aspect by the background of swamps and their malignant fauna – especially alligators and snakes. The result is not to be recommended to the faint-hearted.'
Monthly Film Bulletin

'Bogged down in clichés and apathy.'
Los Angeles Examiner

CREDITS

Swamp Women (US 1956)
pc Bernard Woolner Production
p Bernard Woolner   w David Stern
d Roger Corman   bw
ph Fred West   m Willis Holman
ed Ronald Sinclair
66 mins
Cast: Carole Matthews (Lee), Touch (Mike) Connors (Bob), Berverly Garland (Vera), Marie Windsor (Josie), Jil Jarmyn (Billie), Susan Cummings (Marie), Lou Place, Jonathan Haze, Ed(ward) Nelson

'Good science fiction thriller.'

'I found Roger, or Rog as we used to call him, as hard working as a stevedore and as honest as the day was long. But he tended to overlook the details that make the difference between a great film like *Frankenstein* and just an okay one like *Tarantula*. Rog was obsessed with the idea of making a picture as fast as possible and slamming it out. And this was obvious to anyone who ever worked under his direction.'
Paul Blaisdell

To my way of thinking, I never made a 'B' movie in my life' but the truth is that movie-goers as opposed to movie critics and buffs were beginning to hail him as such. Corman went on to capitalize on the success of Day the World Ended *by making two low-budget science fiction classics,* Not of this Earth *and* It Conquered the World *and one legendary mutant monster movie,* Attack of the Crab Monsters.

Backstory

Corman shot *Not of This Earth* in two weeks for under $100,000: the addition of tongue-in-cheek humour helped it gross almost $1 million. Miller dressed for his comic role as a door-to-door vacuum cleaner salesman in a black cashmere coat and black shirt and shrugged off Corman's concerns by claiming he had dressed that way while working as a salesman in the Bronx. 'When I

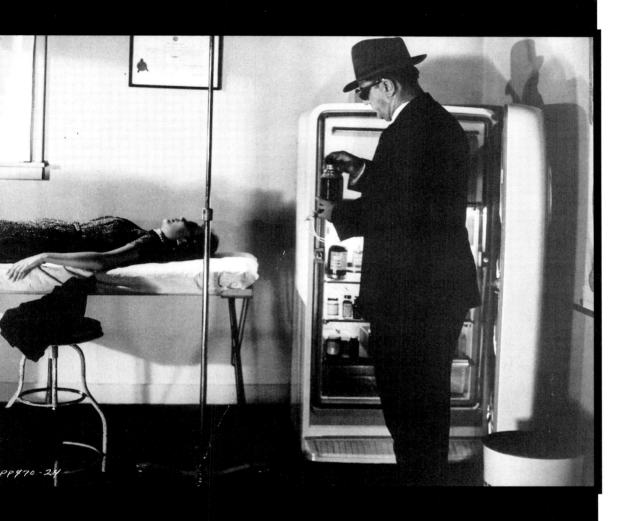

PP470-24

Not of This Earth
Blood theft — by aliens

started singing in the basement when we were filming, Corman yelled – "What are you doing?!" I was doing Jackie Gleason. "Oh, that's interesting", he says. And that about sums up my relationship with Roger,' said Miller. 'Everything I did he would say, "Oh, that's interesting".' Corman's fast-shooting technique upset Birch who was already unhappy at having to wear painful contact lenses for long periods and who, according to Garland felt that working in a low-budget film was somewhat below him. He eventually quit and Corman used a double to complete his scenes.

Garland, however, understood the rules of the game and commented, 'When you work with Roger Corman, there isn't time to think – I mean you'd do it and do it fast and you better know your crap and you better get in there and get it done. That's the way Roger is.'

Corman cut his usual budgetary corners, giving Blaisdell little time or money to come up with the 'Teleportation Portal' (made from balsa wood and decorated with flashing lights), Birch's 'Blood Suitcase' which was simply a customized commercial case and the two-inch high *Space Patrol* 'Marksman' figure that stood in for the Controller of Davanna. 'But,' said Blaisdell, 'wouldn't we all like to see it done better if we didn't have to have it ready 'yesterday' for Rog?'

Story

A humanoid alien comes to Earth and kills people with his eyes before sending their blood to his home planet of Davanna to save its population whose blood is evaporating.

Corman leavens his space-vampire shocker with well-integrated black comedy to excellent effect in the best of his genre B features: the concept of a humanoid alien in a dark suit and glasses who resembles a minor civil servant until he takes off his glasses to reveal his blank, lethal eyes and who dies mundanely in a car smash comes off well. Monster fans are (briefly) catered for by Paul Blaisdell's embryo and adult extraterrestrials and by the flying creature that kills William Roerick.

Reviews

'Good science fiction thriller. The out-of-this-world science-fiction flavour of *Not of this Earth* makes it a handy entry for exploitation playdates generally... Roger Corman production... Corman also directs the script by Charles B Griffith and Mark Hanna. It plays off at a regulation pace with attention to chills and thrills... things get gory, but science fiction fans won't mind. They should like the ending because, just as the scout has been laid to rest, fadeout finds another arrival to continue the work... the cast does all that is required by the story and its screen development.'
Variety

'... offers something new in the way of preparation for the invasion of Earth by people from outer space. It is a macabre story with some gruesome and horrific moments, these being particularly provided by scenes in which the stranger removes his glasses to betray horrible eyes that can kill at a glance. The picture maintains a fair level of tension and thrills, relieved by just a slight romantic element and occasional touches of humour, and makes reliable entertainment where the type is popular.'
CEA Film Report

'This grisly little tale, falling into a division between horror and science fiction, introduces one or two relatively original variations on the macabre. Since the film shows such a marked improvement on *Attack of the Crab Monsters* (made by substantially the same team) one hopes it is the more recent of the two films.'
Monthly Film Bulletin (1957)

'Fine acting by veteran Paul Birch and neat suspense-filled pace, photography et al belie economy of notorious cost-conscious director Roger Corman.'
Castle of Frankenstein

CREDITS ❯❯❯❯❯❯❯❯❯❯❯❯❯❯❯❯❯

Not of This Earth (US 1956)
pc Los Altos. For Allied Artists
w Charles B Griffith, Mark Hanna
bw.
sfx Paul Blaisdell
mu Curly Batson
67 mins.
p, d Roger Corman
ph John Mesacll
ed Charles Gross Jr.
m Ronald Stein
title artwork Paul Julian

Cast: Paul Birch (Paul Johnson/Alien), Beverly Garland (Nadine Story), Morgan Jones (Harry Sherbourne), William Roerick (Dr Rochelle), Dick Miller (Joe Piper), Pat Flynn (Officer Simmons), Jonathan Haze (Jeremy Perrin), Ann Carol (Woman from Davanna), Roy Engel (Sergeant Walton), Gail Ganley, Ralph Reed (Teenagers), Harold Fong (Chinese Victim)

IT CONQUERED THE WORLD

'This flying saucer pic is a definite cut above normal.'

You know, when you work with Roger Corman, there isn't time to think — I mean you'd do it and do it fast and you better know your crap aand you better get in there and get it done. That's the way Roger is.
Beverly Garland

Despite its exploitative title, *It Conquered the World* covers similar concepts of loss of personality to a totalitarian force as the same year's *Invasion of the Body Snatchers*.

Backstory

The screenplay was rewritten and completed in three days by an uncredited Charles B Griffith when Lou Russoff, whose brother was ill, was unable to finish it. Griffith also appeared briefly in front of the camera as a scientist.

Corman used his knowledge of physics and engineering and came up with the entirely logical concept that the alien would be short and squat because of the larger gravitational pull of Venus. Unfortunately, when Garland first saw the stunted creature she sneered, 'So you've come to conquer the world have you? Well, take *that*!' and kicked it. Result — the alien was (illogically) rebuilt ten feet tall and Corman formulated his First Law of Screen Shock: 'Always make the monster bigger than your leading lady.'

Paul Blaisdell, who believed the creature, which he called 'Beulah' would be of vegetable origin because Venus was considered to be hot and damp and therefore more conducive to vegetable life, built Beulah of foam rubber over a wooden skeleton, with latex antennae, carved pine teeth and flashlights which made the eyes glow.

He also constructed working pincers which were wrecked on the first day of shooting when grips ran over the arms while they were resting on the ground and almost crushed them. Blaisdell, who played the visitor from Venus, could still raise the arms but the claws no longer worked. The effect of Beulah's melting eye was achieved cheaply using chocolate syrup. He also created the four 'bat-mites' (nicknamed 'Manny', 'Moe', 'Mack' and 'Sleepy') which were flown over the action on wires.

In Britain *It Conquered the World* earned an X (adults only) certificate but only after producer Samuel Z Arkoff had personally assured the then censor John Trevelyan as to Beulah's out-of-this-world provenance. 'I realised something about the British,' said Arkoff in 1991. 'They have a very high regard for animals, and a very low regard for humans. So I said to him, 'Well, of *course*! This is a human being!'. He said, 'It doesn't *look* like a human being!' I said, 'It's a human being from this

other world!' So he passed the picture. And if we had said it was an animal, the picture would never have played in England.'

Story

An idealistic scientist guides a Venusian to the Earth where it proceeds to take over the humans' minds using bizarre flying 'bat-mites' which turn them into emotionless slaves.

Typically zestful low budget Fifties science fiction shocker whose taut, economical direction and good acting help compensate for one of the more ludicrous-looking extraterrestrials – a giant vegetable marrow with teeth and a very bad attitude – in the celluloid bestiary.

Reviews

'This flying saucer pic is a definite cut above normal, and should help pull its weight at b.o., despite modest budget. However, militating against this are a number of fairly gruesome sequences which producer-director Roger Corman has injected. The Lou Russoff screenplay poses some remarkably adult questions among the derring-do... Director Roger Corman does a generally good job of mingling the necessary background-setting with fast-paced dialogue, to achieve the strongest impact. Only a few patches of abstract discussion fail to hold audience attention ... Producer Corman would have been wiser merely to suggest the creature, rather than construct the awesome-looking and mechanically clumsy rubberized horror. It inspired more titters than terror.'
Variety

'Although the production values of this film are unpolished, it makes quite good entertainment of its kind since it maintains a lively pace throughout, it has some genuinely macabre moments and a good measure of thrills of an unsophisticated order. The film makes reliable entertainment for followers of science-fiction and 'horror' films. It is competently acted.'
CEA Film Report

'Roger Corman's production is well integrated with science fact and fantasy for enough believability to maintain interest and excitement.'
The Hollywood Reporter

'May call down the wrath of groups concerned with kiddie pix fare. But it must be admitted that the packed house of moppets at the show caught appeared to relish the gore.'
Daily Variety

'Compared with previous small budget science fiction films, *It Conquered the World* presents its horrors in a reasonably convincing manner. Although the film's production values are modest, the acting weak and the dialogue naïvely pretentious, the total effect is quite exciting, the central idea (which bears some resemblance to the superior *Invasion of the Body Snatchers*) being developed with some lively invention.'
Monthly Film Bulletin

'Fair, fast-moving little SF thriller. Loveable cucumber-creature from space.'
Castle of Frankenstein

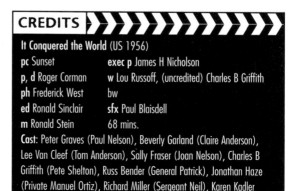

CREDITS ▶▶▶▶▶▶▶▶▶▶▶▶▶▶

It Conquered the World (US 1956)

pc Sunset	**exec p** James H Nicholson
p, d Roger Corman	**w** Lou Russoff, (uncredited) Charles B Griffith
ph Frederick West	bw
ed Ronald Sinclair	**sfx** Paul Blaisdell
m Ronald Stein	68 mins.

Cast: Peter Graves (Paul Nelson), Beverly Garland (Claire Anderson), Lee Van Cleef (Tom Anderson), Sally Fraser (Joan Nelson), Charles B Griffith (Pete Shelton), Russ Bender (General Patrick), Jonathan Haze (Private Manuel Ortiz), Richard Miller (Sergeant Neil), Karen Kadler (Ellen Peters), Paul Blaisdell (Visitor from Venus)

ATTACK OF THE CRAB MONSTERS

'It isn't believable but it's fun.'

Someone once said that Roger could make a film in a phone booth for the cost of a call to New York and finish it before the three minutes were up. And that wasn't even much of an exaggeration.
Sam Arkoff

Radiation was the cause of the majority of giant monster movies that stampeded through cinemas in the Fifties, notably the seminal *Them!* (1954) and rather less noteworthy examples such as *X The Unknown/The Creeping Unknown* (1956), *The Monster that Challenged the World* (1957), *Beginning of the End* (1957), *The Amazing Colossal Man* (1956), *The Cyclops* (1957). *Attack of the Crab Monsters* was Corman's lively contribution to the genre.

Backstory

Attack of the Crab Monsters was shot on Leo Carrillo State Beach, cost $70,000 and took more than $1 million at the box-office which made it Corman's most profitable picture to date. 'I think', said Corman, 'its success had something to do with the wildness of the title... (and) with the construction of the storyline.' Future *Peyton Place* star Ed Nelson made his visible acting debut and was also under the carapace, helping operate the crab, along with Corman's key grip Chuck Hanawalt and other crew members.

Griffith also doubled as director of the underwater sequences after making Corman an offer (he would do it for $100) he couldn't refuse. Unfortunately for

Griffith, the crab was stuffed with Styrofoam which prevented it from sinking so that it had to be weighed down with to keep it below the surface. Actor Mel Welles claimed that, 'They tried winching it under the water, and it exploded.'

Story

Scientists investigating the disappearance of missing colleagues on a remote Pacific island find the place is becoming smaller as a result of landslides due to explosions caused by 25-foot mutant crabs which eat humans, assimilate their intelligence and then mimic their voices to bring themselves further nourishment.

Zestful B feature science fiction shocker with a rather more interesting premise than many of its contemporaries, in spite of the less-than-convincing crustaceans. Corman's instruction to writer Griffiths was 'I want suspense or action in every scene. Audiences must feel something could happen at any time', and it paid off handsomely, putting its stock characters through almost as many perils as Pauline.

Reviews

'It isn't believable, but it's fun as scripted by associate producer Charles Griffith and put on film by Corman and his cast.'
Variety

'... apart from some fairly successfully contrived trick shots, the film has little to offer. The story is muddled and scrappy; much of the explanation of the events which occur is hazy and, even when intelligible, unduly extravagant; the thrills often fail to materialize as they

should and, instead, fall flat; the cast is unprepossessing and the acting rather weak. A few touches of mild spectacle are provided by some landslide scenes and by the sequences in which the crabs figure.'
CEA Film Report

'Average... suffers from a limited budget so that the monsters that provide the chief horror... are not as large or menacing as they should be.'
The Hollywood Reporter

'A below average exemplar of the current science-fiction vogue. The story is chaotic, the idea is wildly over-exploited and the film in general verges on the lunatic, with remarkably poor playing.'
Monthly Film Bulletin

'Gruesome mediocre sf-horror.'
Castle of Frankenstein

CREDITS >>>>>>>>

Attack of the Crab Monsters (US 1957)
pc Los Altos   **p, d** Roger Corman
w Charles B Griffith   **ph** Floyd Crosby
bw   **ed** Charles Gross Jr.
m Ronald Stein   **mu** Curley Batson
62 mins.

Cast: Richard Garland (Dale Drewer), Pamela Duncan (Martha Hunter), Russell Johnson (Hank Chapman), Leslie Bradley (Dr Karl Weigand), Mel Welles (Jules Deveroux), Richard Cutting (Dr James Carson), Beech Dickerson (Ron Fellows), Tony Miller (Jack Somers), Ed Nelson (Ensign Quinlan)

Attack of the Crab Monsters
1957 A large crab set to attack with Ed Nelson lurking within

SHE-GODS OF SHARK REEF

'Fine colour, rich red blood, capable underwater photography and very little story.'

I'm not a pure artist by any means, but I'm not a pure business-man either; I'm a little of both, and, being that way, I can make movies the way I think they should be made – on low budgets.
Roger Corman

The success of *Attack of the Crab Monsters* confirmed Corman's conviction that combining horror and humour could be made to pay off and he would go on to prove it again with *A Bucket of Blood*, *The Last Woman on Earth* and *The Little Shop of Horrors*. Rather than take a vacation, he embarked on a working holiday by making two pictures back-to-back in Hawaii: the first was *She Gods of Shark Reef*.

Backstory
Corman saved money for lawyer-producer Ludwig Gerber by using Hawaii to stand in for the South Seas and by sharing the production overheads with AIP for whom he made *Thunder over Hawaii* after he completed *She-Gods of Shark Reef* in under two weeks on a budget of less than $100,000.

Corman also further trimmed expenses by negotiating a cut-price accommodation deal with the Cocoa Palms Hotel on the island of Kauai in exchange for on-screen promotion.

Story
A killer and his brother are shipwrecked on a South Sea island inhabited only by pearl-diving women, one of whom falls for the good brother who saves her from being sacrificed: the bad brother is eaten by sharks while trying to escape with stolen pearls.

Hearty action rather than a convincing storyline or credible characters categorises this undemanding essay in colourful adventure hokum.

Reviews
'Boasts fine colour, rich red blood, capable underwater photography and very little story... (Durant and Cord) both appear on the screen for the first time, and the credit for two performances that, if not highly professional, are at least believable, goes to director Roger Corman... Carol Lindsay does a whoppingly good hula.'
Variety

'Only the simplest tastes are catered for in this artificial tale of Hawaiian villainies ... melodramatic framework allows for some commonplace underwater swimming and an attack on a synthetic shark, but otherwise there seems little action or even incident beyond a tepid sacrificial offering of a maiden to the island gods, and the phoney encounter with the shark in the climax. On the mildly spectacular side, the local maidens stage a hula-hula wiggle-waggle, and the excellent colour photography of lovely island settings is worthy of a better entertainment caper. The portrayal is resolutely competent... only mild entertainment for uncritical audiences.'
CEA Film Report

'Some lush and bizarre exteriors, beautifully shot in Eastman Colour, have been thrown away on a poor

script, indifferently performed. Apart from such conventional attractions as sharks, a fight between two brothers and a hula dance, the film's liveliest moments come from Dua, as game and energetic an old matriarch as one could wish for.'
Monthly Film Bulletin

CREDITS

She-Gods of Shark Reef
(GB: Shark Reef) (US 1957)
pc James D Radford Productions/AIP   **p** Ludwig H Gerber
d Roger Corman   **w** Robert Hill, Victor Stoloff
ph Floyd Crosby   colour
ed Frank Sullivan   **m** Ronald Stein
song Nearer **My Love To You** by Jack Lawrence & Frances Hall,
sung by Sylvia Sims   **mu** Curly Batson
63 mins.
Cast: Don Durant (Lee), Bill Cord (Chris), Lisa Montell (Mahia),
Jeanne Gerson (Dua), Carol Lindsay (Hula Dancer), **Roger Corman**
(Plantation Administrator)

She-Gods of Shark Reef
1957 Horror and humour pay off

NAKED PARADISE / THUNDER OVER HAWAII

'Colorful Hawaiian melodrama which may be exploited for good returns.'

Roger made us work hard and long. I remember that. He was always fascinating to me, a fascinating man and a good businessman! He had such incredible energy, it was tremendous.
Beverly Garland

Having completed *She-Gods of Shark Reef*, Corman immediately segued into making *Thunder over Hawaii* for AIP.

Backstory

Corman's deal with the Cocoa Palms Hotel on Kauai which gave him excellent rates in exchange for an on-screen credit meant that, for once, Garland (who was making her last film for him) did not have to rough it on location. 'Roger really did this one up the right way', she said, 'I don't know if it was because we were at this beautiful location and Roger simply felt like spending more, but it was one of the best locations ever – especially for a Roger Corman film.'

Corman filmed genuine sugarcane field fires to give *Thunder Over Hawaii* more spectacle than his $100,000 could afford and further economised by giving himself the role of a plantation owner who is stabbed to death during a safe robbery.

AIP Vice-President Arkoff who was in Hawaii with his family was also recruited to appear in front of the camera. 'Roger told me one day to come over to where he was shooting, and he gave me this one line to read to Richard Denning: "It's been a good harvest, and the money is in the safe." Now *that's* a key line. That was my first and last role.'

Story

A criminal charters a schooner to make his getaway with his two henchmen and his girlfriend after robbing Hawaiian plantation owners but the boat's skipper foils their escape and wins the girl.

Corman effectively disguises the inadequacies of the sometimes confused script with muscular action, a spectacular fire and attractive Hawaiian locations.

Reviews

'Colourful Hawaiian melodrama which may be exploited for good returns. Interesting action and scenery lensed in elegant Pathecolor backdrop, this melodrama... producer-director Roger Corman uses the natural beauties of the Islands to excellent advantage in his unfolding of a well-knit story... considerable violence crops up occasionally to give rather grim overtones to the action, but this is legitimately inserted and is a natural plot development ... Corman helms his characters convincingly and all principals come up with above-average performances.'
Variety

'It is difficult to follow the narrative intricacies of this unconvincing, complicated and violent story... it might be that these very modest action highlights will pass muster with the uncritical, but otherwise the picture has little to offer in the way of coherent entertainment. Poor direction does nothing to aid a chaotic script, while the acting is merely adequate to the simple requirements.'
CEA Film Report

'This is a straightforward romantic adventure, with good and beautiful savages, wicked white men and appropriate sadistic incidents such as the fishing of a man out of the sea by a harpoon hook through his shoulder. Floyd Crosby, the past-master of exotic camerawork, injects a suitable romantic atmosphere, and the film relies on its settings rather than anything exciting in the way of action. Of its kind, it is adequately realised and played.'
Monthly Film Bulletin

CREDITS

Naked Paradise/Thunder Over Hawaii (US 1956)

pc Roger Corman Productions
p, d Roger Corman
ph Floyd Crosby
ed Charles Gross Jr.
m Ronald Stein
68 mins.

exec p James H Nicholson
w Charles B Griffith, Mark Hanna
colour. WideVision
wardrobe Shaheen of Honolulu
Hawaiian songs Alvin Kaleolani

Cast: Richard Denning (Duke), Beverly Garland (Max), Lisa Montell (Keena), Leslie Bradley (Zac), Richard Miller (Mitch), Jonathan Haze (Stony), Roger Corman (Plantation administrator), Samuel Z Arkoff (Plantation owner)

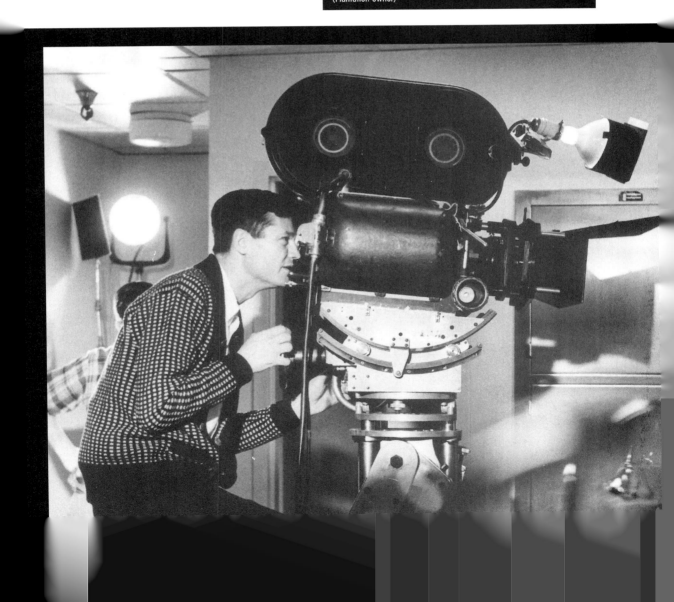

'Low grade stuff attempts to cop a fast-buck ride on music fad.'

He was eager to try new things in those days and he was very, very decisive. That's what made him a great low-budget picture maker. He could make a decision instantly if time was being wasted or money was flying out the window.
Mel Welles

When Arkoff and Nicholson decided to add juvenile delinquent melodramas to their roster of movies aimed at the teenage drive-in cinema audiences, Corman once again switched genres and made three teen-oriented pictures in 1957, two of them for AIP. *Rock all Night* was the first.

Back story

Corman had Griffith revamp and expand the source material, a 25-minute television show *The Little Guy*, changing the setting from a bar to a rock and roll club. 'Chuck, with my advice, wrote the part for a character *I* used to write for – Lord Buckley,' said Welles. 'He was a comedian who has a large cult following, even today. He was the first one to do 'hip' talk... Sir Bop was written for him. Then he disappeared somewhere, so I played it myself – dyed my hair silver and tried to do him the best I could.' Corman shot *Rock All Night* (which, like *Day the World Ended*, set out to examine a motley group of people under psychological pressure) on a single set in seven days, one of which was spent filming The Platters as they lip-synched two numbers. To finish the film on schedule, Corman would take only a lunch break, carry on filming until dinner and then spend time planning the next day's work.

Story

Two killers who shoot a witness in a rock and roll bar, hold the patrons hostage and force a singer to perform to jukebox tracks to lull the suspicions of passers-by, are taunted by an aggressive barfly into surrendering to the police without a fight.

Corman and AIP's attempt to jump on the *Rock Around the Clock* bandwagon is a bizarre blend of music and melodrama redeemed by Miller's performance and, for those who enjoy their music, The Platters.

Reviews

'Low grade stuff attempts to cop a fast-buck ride on music fad. Here's a weirdie – of the order of *Time of Your Life* – to the rhythm of rock 'n' roll. Extremely mediocre and drawing unintended guffaws... only the performance (very good, especially considering the so-so production and direction) of Dick Miller in the lead keeps the audience's interest in the film from disintegrating.'
Variety

'Luckily, this film is short, and frequently interrupted by indifferent rock 'n' roll, rhythm or blues numbers that make no demand on the attention. The story and characters are pure comic-strip material, and the script is a succession of uninspired wise-cracks. The title is an attempt to cash in on the current craze; but rock 'n' roll addicts will find little here to "send" them.'
Monthly Film Bulletin

Rock All Night
A teen love and music pic

CREDITS ➤➤➤➤➤➤➤➤➤➤➤➤➤➤➤

Rock All Night (US 1957)
pc AIP   p, d Roger Corman
w Charles Griffith   ph Floyd Crosby
bw   ed Frank Sullivan
ad Robert Kinoshita   m Buck Ram
62 mins.
Cast: Dick Miller (Shorty), Abby Dalton (Julie), Robin Morse (Al),
Richard Cutting (Steve), Bruno Ve Sota (Charlie), Chris Alcaide
(Angie), Mel Welles (Sir Bop), Barboura Morris (Syl), Clegg Hoyt
(Marty), (Russell Johnson (Jigger), Jonathan Haze (Joey), Richard
Karlan (Jerry), Jack DeWitt (Bartender), Beech Dickerson (The Kid),
Ed Nelson (Pete), The Platters (Themselves), The Block Busters
(Themselves)

Sorority Girl
1957 Susan Cabot has teenage angst

SORORITY GIRL

We would have some sort of a script, but there was a lot of 'Who's going to say what?' and 'How 'bout I do this?' – plenty of ad-libbing and improvising. Roger was really great in a way; he was very loose. If something didn't work out, he changed it right away.
Susan Cabot

Backstory

'This picture taught me when to go for the close-up', said Corman. 'It was one of those movies that you say you learn a lesson from. I learned the hard way on this film that if the script isn't right, you shouldn't shoot.' He had been impressed by Cabot's work in *Carnival Rock* and gave her the lead, only to find while shooting a key scene between her and her uncaring mother that the Method-trained New York actress had given her all in the first take and had nothing to draw on for the subsequent close up. This experience led Corman to enrol with dramatic coach Jeff Corey in order to learn how actors tick. The classes also introduced him to actor Jack Nicholson and screenwriter Robert Towne, both of whom later worked for him.

Story

A teenage college student with emotional problems gives her fellow sorority members a hard time.

An overheated campus exploitation melodrama with an uneasy script... well acted by Cabot: the inventive opening credits are almost the most interesting aspect of the film.

Reviews

'Routine cheapie with better acting than production warrants. *Sorority Girl* is a sombre affair... although the pic's low budget is all too apparent, film should draw curious teenagers in its bookings with *Motorcycle Gang*.

Storyline is a good one... with more care than is shown in this pic, results could have been good. Susan Cabot displayed a few bursts of acting talent... on the whole, however, her role as written is without sufficient motivation...'
Variety

'Here is another tale of depravity in communities where young girls are herded together... the sordid type of background often customary with this type of film is abandoned in favour of quite luxurious and decidedly modern college settings, even though at no time during the course of the picture is there even a hint of the existence of any classrooms or of work being done!... though the settings are not sordid, the action is far from wholesome. Despite its short length, the picture is slow moving with dull patches, but at best it is weak entertainment of an unpleasant kind and is likely to hold only moderate appeal for those teenagers attracted to this kind of picture.'
CEA Film Report

'A contrived little melodrama determinedly planned as a teenage shocker. Almost its only asset is Susan Cabot's performance as the 'Bad One' of the English title; overcoming a good deal of juvenile dialogue, she makes Sabra's viciousness surprisingly credible and even manages to win some sympathy for her.'
Monthly Film Bulletin

CREDITS ▶▶▶▶▶▶▶▶▶▶▶

Sorority Girl (US 1957) (GB: **The Bad One**)
pc Roger Corman Productions
w Ed Waters, Leo Lieberman
bw
m Ronald Stein
60 mins.
p, d Roger Corman
ph Monroe P Askins
ed Charles Gross Jr
titles Bill Martin
Cast: Susan Cabot (Sabra Tanner), Dick Miller (Mort), Barboura O'Neill (Rita Joyce), June Kenny (Tina), Barbara Crane (Billie Marshall), Fay Barker (Mrs Tanner), Jeane Wood (Mrs Fessenden)

CARNIVAL ROCK

'Overtones of Pagliacci and out-and-out rock 'n' roll...'

I had never seen such cost-cutting as Roger Corman did. But there was no question that that guy really knew what he was doing – he was miraculous at turning out acceptable product in no time at all.
Anthony Eisley

Corman made his other two 1957 low-budget teen pics, *Carnival Rock* and *Teenage Doll*, for Howco International and Allied Artists respectively.

Story

A one-time burlesque comic-turned-nightclub owner loves his singer but she loves a gambler who wins ownership of the club. The former owner stays on and performs between the acts until the couple marry and he is dismissed.

The music is better than the storyline and screenplay; the acting is adequate.

Reviews

'Overtones of Pagliacci and out-and-out rock 'n' roll have been mixed together by producer-director Roger Corman ... film has a couple of very good performances in Susan Cabot and Dick Miller ... Corman did an okay job as producer, and, for the most part, as director.'
Variety

CREDITS ▶▶▶▶▶▶▶▶▶▶▶▶▶▶

Carnival Rock (US 1957)
pc Howco International
p, d Roger Corman
ph Floyd Crosby
ed Charles Gross Jr.
m Walter Greene, Buck Ram
A Roger Corman Production
b Leo Lieberman
bw
p des Robert Kinoshita
75 mins.
Cast: Susan Cabot (Natalie), Brian Hutton (Stanley), David J Stewart (Christy), Dick Miller (Ben) Iris Adrian (Celia), Jonathan Haze (Max), Ed Nelson (Cannon), Chris Alcaide (Slug), Horace Logan (M.C.), Yvonne Peattie (Mother), Gary Hunley (Boy), Frankie Ray (Billy), Dorothy Neuman (Clara), Clara Andressa (Cleaning lady #1), Terry Blake (Cleaning Lady #2): with the music of The Platters, David Houston, Bob Luman, The Shadows, The Blockbusters

LE CHÂTEAU HANTÉ

d'après **EDGAR ALLAN POE**

**VINCENT PRICE
DEBRA PAGET
LON CHANEY**

Régie ROGER CORMAN

HET SPOOKKASTEEL

TEENAGE DOLL

'Another juve delinquency cheapie.'

Every page of the script was rejected by the censors and I had to write it over again during the weekend.
Charles B Griffith

Backstory

'What we tried to do was touch on as many contemporary topics as possible within the given framework. In this film , we managed to touch on both gang warfare and the rivalry between the classes in the suburbs,' said Corman.

Producer Bernard Woolner (who owned drive-in cinemas in Louisiana) supplied the title, Charles Griffith supplied the standard script and Corman brought the film in ten days. When Corman was shooting exteriors in West Hollywood the woman in the next door house turned on her sprinklers, hoping to pressure him into paying her to turn them off. Corman won the skirmish by telling her he would only pay if the sprinklers were left on all night to add visual interest. She switched them off.

Story

A young female gang member knifes a member of a rival gang and is hunted by the dead girl's vengeful gang.

Corman certainly packs plenty of action into a relatively short running-time and maintains a fast pace but otherwise there is little to differentiate *Teenage Doll* from other similar 1950s juvenile delinquent exploitation offerings.

Reviews

'Another juve delinquency cheapie. Clumsily executed For the sex-and-sadism fanciers. This low-budgeter is ostensibly directed toward the fight against juve delinquency. However, the only real contribution in this direction is that it offers employment to corps of juve actors, and thus off the street, if not precisely gainfully occupied. More and more, these delinquent pix, tailore strictly for the exploitation market despite their pious declarations, are beginning to display a deadening monotonous sameness. As a famed producer once observed, 'It's time to develop some new clichés'. Unremitting and unconvincing downbeat tenor, clums ly executed, deadens b.o. chances for any audience outside of sex-and-sadism fanciers. Characters in Charles Griffith screenplay talk a stylized jargon mainly derivative of other pix of this genre; engage in continual bru tality and violence; and their motivations, delinquent o otherwise, bear only the slightest resemblance to huma beings... Direction of Roger Corman, who also produced, stresses an array of facial gymnastics rarely seen since silent screen days. He sticks in several scenes of tasty young dishes in various states of deshabillé, with little discernible relation to the plot. However, to Corman's credit, he does show an ability to assemble t production ingredients for a good picture, even it he doesn't know what to do with them.'
Variety

Teenage Doll
1957 Gang warfare and the rivalry between the classes in the suburbs.

CREDITS ►►►►►►►►►►►►►►►►►

Teenage Doll (US 1957)
pc A Woolner Brothers Production   **exec p** Bernard Woolner
assoc p Lawrence Woolner   **p, d** Roger Corman
w Charles B Griffith   **ph** Floyd Crosby
bw   **ed** Charles Gross
ad Robert Kinoshita   **m** Walter Greene
67 mins.
Cast: June Kenney (Barbara), Fay Spain (Hel), John Brinkley (Eddie),
Collette Jackson (May), Barbara Wilson (Betty), Ziva Rodan
(Squirrel), Sandy Smith (Lorrie), Barboura Morris (Janet), Richard
Devon (Dunston), Jay Sayer (Wally), Richard Cutting (Phil), Dorothy
Neumann (Estelle), Ed Nelson (Dutch Doctor), Bruno Ve Sota

THE UNDEAD

Roger never did another take unless it was absolutely impossible to get around a mistake. If something went wrong or if a take was blown or something like that, what he used to do was give it to the editor, and use some footage to cut around.
Richard Devon

Corman returned to horror with *The Undead* which he conceived to cash in on the current vogue for reincarnation which had been catalysed by the popularity of the best-seller *The Search for Bridey Murphy*.

Backstory

'We're talking $70,000 on a ten-day schedule', recalled Corman in 1991. *The Undead* was conceived to cash in on the popularity of the reincarnation best-seller *The Search for Bridey Murphy* (filmed in 1956 by writer-director Noel Langley) and Griffith wrote a script called *The Trance of Diana Love* with 'mediaeval' dialogue in iambic pentameters.

Unfortunately, people who read the script did not understand it and Corman had Griffith 'translate it into English'. The interiors were filmed on a small sound stage built in an abandoned supermarket on Sunset Boulevard, renting the sets, props and costumes (one of the latter turned out to be a shirt once worn by Tyrone Power).

'He didn't like to rent anything', noted Griffith. 'You could see the zipper on the witch's dress and all the gimmicks were very obvious and phoney – Roger deliberately played to skid row, a degenerate audience.' The exteriors were shot at the 'Witches Cottage', an exotic 1930s house in Beverly Hills where Corman took care in framing his shots to exclude anything from the twentieth century. There was one recurring theme – actors who had to suffer for Corman's art. 'We almost died of asphyxiation from all the creosote fog', said Welles and Ve Sota complained that the smudge pots used to create fog on the sound stage had caused everybody's eyes to run, and the actors to choke, adding, 'The only person who didn't act like he was affected by all that smoke was Roger Corman. He was already counting the money the picture was going to make.' Devon was even more unhappy. 'His (Corman's) temper was something really quite awesome', he said. 'Someone had left one of my speeches out of the script, so naturally I couldn't learn what wasn't there. And he was not just upset, he was maniacal... You would meet him in his office and he was absolutely charming ... then you would get him on the set and he was Attila the Hun. With Roger, if anything cost more than he had figured, it was a disaster for everybody around him.'

Story

A young call girl is hypnotised by a psychologist and relives her past life as a mediaeval witch.

Corman's entertaining low-budget take on reincarnation and witchcraft gets by on style and speed, the special effects come off satisfactorily and it is never dull.

Reviews

'Minor league horror programmer. A retrogression theme and bosomy dames are used in this ... horror subject as ballyhooed pegs for quickie play dates... the pacing is slow and the thrills at a minimum... lensing by William Sickner, special effects, background score and other technical aids are okay for the budget and quick shooting schedule.'
Variety

The Undead
1957 Someone's about to get the chop

CREDITS ▶▶▶▶▶▶▶▶▶▶▶▶▶

The Undead (US 1957)
pc Balboa   **p, d** Roger Corman
w Charles B Griffith, Mark Hanna   **ph** William Sickner
bw   **ed** Frank Sullivan
m Ronald Stein   **75** mins.
Cast: Pamela Duncan (Diana Love/Helene), Richard Garland
(Pendragon), Allison Hayes (Livia), Val Dufour (Quintus Ratcliff), Mel
Welles (Smolkin), Dorothy Neumann (Meg-Maud), Billy Barty (Imp),
Bruno Ve Sota (Scroop), Aaron Saxon (Gobbo), Richard Devon
(Satan), Dick Miller

WAR OF THE SATELLITES

'Confusing space action melo.'

Corman shoots quickly and there's no time wasted on his sets.
William K. Everson

On 4 October 1957, the Soviet Union won the first heat in the space race when they successfully launched their first orbiting satellite Sputnik 1. The United States followed suit by sending Explorer 1 satellite into orbit on 31st January 1958, by which time Corman's *War of the Satellites* had already been released.

Backstory

Corman followed the Warner Bros. tradition of snatching stories from current headlines after special effects expert Jack Rabin offered him a story that exploited the recent launch of the first Russian Sputnik. Corman quickly made a deal with Allied Artists President Steve Broidy to have a script ready in two weeks, shoot the picture in ten days, cut and dub it in four weeks and have it ready for distribution (in the United States it was shown on a double bill with *Attack of the 50ft Woman*) in two months.

'We did it exactly on that schedule, and it was one of those rare times when everything meshed', noted Corman. 'I delivered the picture on the exact date I promised, and they had the advertising campaign ready at the same time. We booked it directly into the theatres, and the picture did very well.'

The economical spaceship interior designed by Dan Haller was, according to Dick Miller, 'four arches; that's all they were, the entire set was arches. You could set them together to make a short hall or set them further apart and make a long hall. At the end of the hall was a

flat – you made a turn. So on our spaceship, you always ran down to the end of the hall and made a turn. That was the entire ship.'

Corman maintained his usual tight budgetary control to the point of playing the Flight Controller. He told me: 'Under the Screen Actors Guild rules at that time, if you had any actor who appeared at the beginning of the picture and at the end of the picture you had to pay him for the entire length of the picture. So you schedule for the money, you try to put your most expensive actors shooting the least amount of time, which means every now and then you are going to be stuck with some little role that starts in the beginning and then doesn't come back until the end. I would play that role myself because I am not going to pay some actor for two weeks when he is just there on day one and day ten – that is *my* role.'

Story

Extraterrestrials take over the corpse of the leading UN rocket scientist in a bid to end human space exploration.

In spite of the efficient direction, some useful performances and competent model work, the muddled script and patently low budget make it a lesser space saga: but at least Corman did beat the United States into space.

Reviews

'Confusing space action melo. A lesser entry for the exploitation market... plot built around a United Nations satellite programme is so contrived and confusing it misses fire completely. Over-talkative script...

characters are so unreal they are mere walk-throughs... Roger Corman produced and directed, utilizing fewer special effects than are normal for a subject of this type. Technical credits are stock.'
Variety

'Unashamed, incredible hokum but acted with fierce intensity, bringing in the United Nations, telescope peeps at cosmic conflict and final denouement with a sexy lunatic above the earth, to supply the conventional thrills. Mainly for youngsters and uncritical fans.'
CEA Film Report

'Topical... with some very good miniature work... give this Roger Corman film a chance to cash in on the exploitation angles... Dick Miller and Susan Cabot have very pleasant screen personalities and, when given a chance, nice acting abilities.'
The Hollywood Reporter

'Reasonably diverting science fantasy, unduly cluttered with international problems and the inevitably brainy

female in the space ship. The production is generally makeshift, but the trick effects work, the atmosphere is occasionally eerie.'
Monthly Film Bulletin

CREDITS

War of the Satellites (US 1957)
pc Allied Artists International/Corman Productions
p, d Roger Corman   **assoc p, st** Irving Block, Jack Rabin
w Lawrence Louis Goldman   **ph** Floyd Crosby
bw   **ed** Irene Morra.
ad Dan Haller
sfx Jack Rabin, Irving Block, Louis DeWitt
m Walter Greene   **mu** Stanley Orr
66 mins.
Cast: Dick Miller (Dave Boyer), Susan Cabot (Sybil Carrington), Richard Devon (Dr Pol Van Ponder), Eric Sinclair (Dr Lazar), Michael Fox (Jason Ibn Akad), Robert Shayne (Colonel Hodgkiss), Bruno Ve Sota (M Lemoine), Jerry Barclay (John Campo), Mitzi McCall (Jay Jay Sayer), John Brinkley, Beach Dickerson (Crewmen), Roger Corman (Ground Controller)

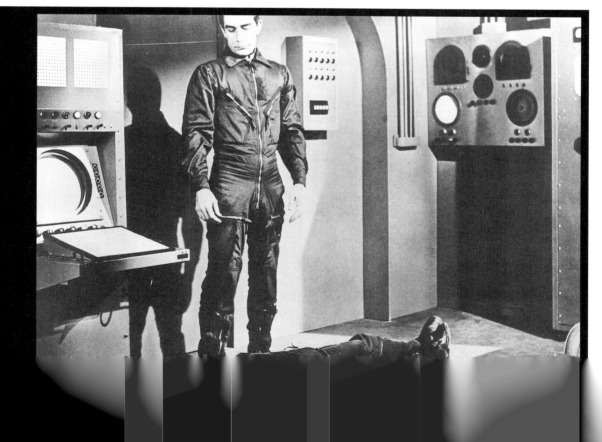

THE VIKING WOMEN AND THE SEA SERPENT

'A wholly preposterous yarn.'

Roger seemed a driven man. Roger wanted to accomplish a lot; he had to have a lot of drive to do it, and he pushed through. He not only pushed through, he punched through. With a lot of energy – and a lot of disregard at times.
Susan Cabot *Fangoria*

Corman did well with *War of the Satellites*. However, when he took up Jack Rabin and Irving Block's offer to create the special effects for a ninth-century Norse sea monster epic, the outcome was disastrous and *The Viking Women and the Sea Serpent* foundered.

Back story

Viking Women, like *War of the Satellites*, had its genesis with Rabin and Block: they had a screenplay and claimed they could bring in the special effects for $110,000. Said Corman: 'They presented me with a series of beautiful drawings of what the monster, the sea serpent, was going to look like and they had the script. I showed them to James Nicholson and he looked at them and he thought "this is wonderful" and I thought it was wonderful. The script was not that good, but we thought it was serviceable and the monster looked great. It wasn't until I came to shoot it that I realised this monster wasn't very good.'

When the originally cast leading lady dropped out, Corman promoted Cabot to leader of the Viking women and made up their number by giving a featured role to her sister who was one of the extras and shot *Viking Women* in ten days on location at the ever useful Bronson Canyon, Cabrillo Beach and the Iverson Ranch. He also achieved a personal record of 77 camera set-ups in a single day.

Once more, Corman's cast had a rough time, as Susan Cabot recalled. 'There were, I believe, 11 girls in a

Viking-type ship, and we were pulled out to sea, tugged by a rope attached to another boat. And the man who was towing us fell asleep! We started screaming at him, but the sound of the ocean drowned us out. Before we knew it, the bottom of our boat began to fill up with water, and we had nothing to bail it out with! I had boots on – I pulled them off and used them to get *some* water out – but all the other girls had sandals. We looked back to the shore, but the crew had already become minutely small in the distance.' They survived the sea only to have to climb a sheer cliff to avoid drowning as the incoming tide covered the beach.

Corman suffered too when Rabin and Block supplied a serpent that in no way matched up to their impressive original presentation. It was too small and they compounded their crime by shooting the process plates from an angle that Corman found impossible to match when he came to stage action in front of them. He did his best by shooting the scene darkly and by using the boat and the women to obscure portions of the back-projected monster.

'The process shots were hilarious', said Dalton, 'They

were rocking the boat in this cavernous studio, squirting hoses and tossing buckets of water at us in our wet Viking buckskins. Between every shot the crew plied us with brandy to keep us from freezing to death.'

'Jim Nicholson was very good at titles', said Corman, 'and I like to work on titles too and we couldn't find a way to bring together the Viking Women and the Sea Serpent in any reasonable way in a title. So finally I said, 'Let's go the other way', and the film became *The Saga of the Viking Women and their Voyage to the Waters of the Great Sea Serpent.* And I went for something I always remembered on the titles. I remember as a kid seeing classics where the camera would be on an ornately embossed leather-bound book, a hand would come in and lift the book and keep turning the pages and there would be a new title on each page. So I thought, I will do exactly that – and it was really looking back to those old MGM pictures.'

Story

Ninth-century Viking women seeking their long-lost husbands are captured by the uncivilised tribe who took their men and when they escape, the eponymous Monster of the Vortex saves them from their pursuers.

The title (especially in full – *The Saga of the Viking Women and Their Voyage to the Waters of the Great Sea Serpent*) is memorable unlike, sadly, the waterlogged proceedings and dire special effects responsible for the (fortunately) barely glimpsed Great Sea Serpent.

Reviews

'A wholly preposterous yarn of Viking women sailing to rescue their captured menfolk, this has plenty of action, but acting is unremarkable and improbabilities pile up at the risk of being unconsciously comic, while much of the dialogue is absurd. The man-hungry Amazons suggest a bevy of leggy American debs in fancy dress and the savage islanders carry little conviction. In fact, average audiences will get quiet fun (if not outright laughs) out of such items as paddling a midget craft through the stormy North Sea with no navigation, lovers at the

burning stake making a date in Valhalla, a barbaric banquet with a dancer by way of a cabaret and an absurd free-for-all, and a short sword killing a vast sea-saurian in a maelstrom. Production seldom escapes the studio touch and as entertainment its mentality is that of 1912. Its appeal is solely to uncritical tastes, but at least it is lively enough.'
CEA Film Report

'In this tale of keen Viking femininity and their luckless males, one character is heard to exclaim, 'You big slob!' A strong sense of anachronism, however, is only one of the absurdities of this attempt to fuse monster-fiction and pre-history. The actors seem to be unaware of their surroundings and act with great gusto, but the sea-serpent is given no more than a walking-on part.'
Monthly Film Bulletin

CREDITS ▶▶▶▶▶▶▶▶▶▶▶▶▶

The Viking Women and the Sea Serpent/
The Saga of the Viking Women and their Voyage to the Waters of the Great Sea Serpent (US 1957)
(GB: Viking Women)

pc Malibu Productions	exec p James H Nicholson
p, d Roger Corman	w Louis Goldman
st Irving Block	ph Monroe P Askins
bw	ed Ronald Sinclair
sfx Jack Rabin and Associates	m Albert Glasser
mu Harry Ross	70 mins.

Cast: Abby Dalton (Desir), Susan Cabot (Enger), Brad Jackson (Vedric), June Kenney (Asmild), Richard Devon (Stark), Betsy Jones-Moreland (Thyra), Jonathan Haze (Ottar), Jay Sayer (Senja), Gary Conway (Jarl)

MACHINE GUN KELLY

'Well-made low budgeter for returns in exploitation market.'

AIP now felt it was time to add gangster pictures to their youth-oriented output and Corman, after producing *Cry Baby Killer* which gave Jack Nicholson one of his first major roles, decided to base his first genre movie on a real-life Public Enemy.

I think he gave a lot of people opportunities to do things they would've never gotten otherwise.
Jonathan Haze *Filmfax*

Backstory

The story of 1930s gangster Machine Gun Kelly particularly appealed to Corman because of his untypical comeuppance. He had given himself up to the FBI agents who had him surrounded and told them: 'I knew if I didn't surrender, you'd kill me.' The inspired casting of 37-year-old character actor Bronson (who was paid $5,000, his largest fee to date) as Kelly paid off handsomely and Corman elicited a powerful portrayal that balanced arrogance and swagger with the weakness he saw as the key to the character. Cabot made a strong impression as Kelly's ruthless and ultimately stronger-willed moll and she thought the film the most satisfactory of her six Corman appearances.

'There was a kind of fun thing going on between the characters of Kelly and Flo – Charles Bronson and myself – and there was a fondness there which came out of the fondness that Bronson and I had for each other,' she recalled. *Machine Gun Kelly* gave Bronson's career a major boost and was shown at film festivals in Europe

where it rightly earned Corman long overdue critical respect, notably in France where the film became a cult and catalyzed French critics' enduring love affair with the director.

Story

The criminal career of notorious 1930s bank robber George R Kelly.

Corman's first gangster picture is tough, taut, sharply characterized, the dialogue hits home and it is excellently acted, especially by Bronson in his first starring role, while Freudians should relish the phallic relationship of Kelly and his eponymous weapon. The jazz score is on target.

Reviews

'Well-made low budgeter for returns in exploitation market. Corman, who produced and directed, has taken a good screenplay by R Wright Campbell, and made a first-rate little picture out of the depressing but intriguing account of a bad man's downfall... *Machine Gun Kelly* and its companion piece (*The Bonnie Parker Story*) should make one of the more profitable exploitation duos of the year... Corman also takes the trouble to sketch briefly but effectively, minor characters and incident that give weight and meaning to the otherwise sordid story. Bronson gives a brooding, taut performance that somehow takes the curse off the character without lessening the horror of the casual slayings.'
Variety

'Convincing, accurate, rapidly paced action-laden films of one of the hardest hombres of this hectic era. For the film's authenticity of atmosphere and circa, as well as its many other superior qualities, much credit is due to energetic Roger Corman.'
Boxoffice

'This is a violent drama of machine-gun gangster mobs and kidnappers in the 1930s. The chief character is a soft-spoken psychopath whose gang notably comprises drunkards and stool pigeons, not to mention his moll who eggs him on and is indeed the worst of the lot. Such sidelines as whisky running and prostitution are hinted at so, what with one thing and another, the film can definitely be termed a 'toughie'. But on the credit side it must be said that the story is neatly told, and told at a cracking pace, too, so that the action, violent and unpleasant though it may be, is almost constant; this, together with one or two believable performances, give the picture punch so that it should make acceptable entertainment where tough gangster fare is popular. Charles Bronson gives an admirable performance in the title role; his evil girl friend is cleverly played by Susan Cabot and the lesser roles are well managed.'
CEA Film Report

'Corman turns ordinary programmer material into vaguely horror-styled manic melodrama... Charles Bronson is forceful as Kelly, and Morey Amsterdam surprisingly good in 'straight' role as 'homo' informer.'
Castle of Frankenstein

CREDITS ▶▶▶▶▶▶▶▶▶▶▶▶▶▶

Machine Gun Kelly (US 1958)
pc AIP	**exec p** Samuel Z Arkoff, James H Nicholson
p, d Roger Corman	**w** R Wright Campbell
ph Floyd Crosby	**bw**
ed Ronald Sinclair	**ad** Daniel Haller
cost Marge Corso	**m** Gerald Fried
mu Dave Newell	84 mins.

Cast: Charles Bronson (Machine Gun Kelly), Susan Cabot (Flo), Morey Amsterdam (Fandango), Jack Lambert (Howard), Wally Campo (Maize), Bob Griffin (Vito), Barboura Morris (Lynn), Richard Devon (Apple), Ted Thorp (Teddy), Mitzi McCall (Harriet), Frank De Kova (Harry), Shirley Falls (Martha), Connie Gilchrist (Ma), Mike Fox (Clinton), Larry Thor (Drummond), George Archambeault (Frank), Jay Sayer (Philip Ashton)

I, MOBSTER

'Well turned-out gangster film.'

After *Machine Gun Kelly* performed well for AIP, Corman segued into his second gangster picture *I Mobster*.

There was nobody better than Roger! He produced and directed four or five pictures a year, he was a hard worker, he always brought them in on budget – which is more than I can say for practically anybody else.
Samuel Z Arkoff

Backstory

Independent producer Edward L Alperson who released his films through 20th Century-Fox came to Corman with the Steve Fisher screenplay for *I, Mobster*. Roger and Gene produced the picture, Steve Cochran gave one of his best performances, although Corman felt the film lacked the depth of *Machine Gun Kelly*.

Story

The rise of a petty racketeer from bookie's runner and drug pusher to crime czar and his eventual elimination by his criminal confederates.

Directed with sufficient vigour to overcome most of the deficiencies of the episodic and conventional script, spiced with welcome touches of gallows humour but lacking the unconventional sharpness of the characterizations and motivations of *Machine Gun Kelly*.

Reviews

'Well turned-out gangster film. *I, Mobster* is a return to the long-absent gangster cycle. It's a well turned-out melodrama with Steve Cochran in the title role delivering a slick characterization of the rise and fall of a mobsman. Dual producership of Roger and Gene Corman is responsible for values which should pay off in the better programme market... under Roger Corman's know-how direction action unfolds smoothly and swiftly. Through very creditable performances, Corman manages to capture the gangster feeling and in addition to Cochran outstanding portrayals are contributed by Lita Milan as

his sweetheart; Strauss, socking over his henchman role after Cochran rises above him; and Celia Lovsky as Cochran's sorely tried mother... technical credits are generally skilfully handled.'
Variety

'Adhering throughout to the well-trodden path of gangster action of the gun menace and beating-up order, this latest slant on the life and death of a hoodlum makes no pretence at novelty. The big shot's rise to omnipotence seems very sketchy in its succession of cold-blooded killings.'
CEA Film Report

'The script and Roger Corman's direction for the most part manage to gloss over the episodic nature of the story and embellish it with several flashes of black humour.'
Monthly Film Bulletin

CREDITS ▶▶▶▶▶▶▶▶▶▶▶▶▶▶

I, Mobster (US 1958) (GB: The Mobster)
pc An Alco Picture   An Edward L Alperson Production
p Gene Corman, Roger Corman   **d** Roger Corman
w Steve Fisher
From the novel by Joseph Hilton Smyth
ph Floyd Crosby   **bw**
ed William B Murphy   **ad** Daniel Haller
cost Marjorie Corso
m Gerald Fried, Edward L Alperson Jr.
songs Give Me Love, Lost, Lonely And Looking For Love
m Edward L Alperson Jr, lyrics Jerry Winn
mu Ted Coodley   80 mins.
Cast: Steve Cochran (Joe Sante), Lita Milan (Teresa Porter), Robert Strauss (Black Frankie Udino), Celia Lovsky (Mrs Sante), Lili St Cyr (Herself), John Brinkley (Ernie Porter), Yvette Vickers (The Blonde), Robert Shayne (Senator), Grant Withers (Joe Moran), Frank Gerstle (District Attorney), Wally Cassell (Cherry-Nose), John Mylong (Mr Sante)

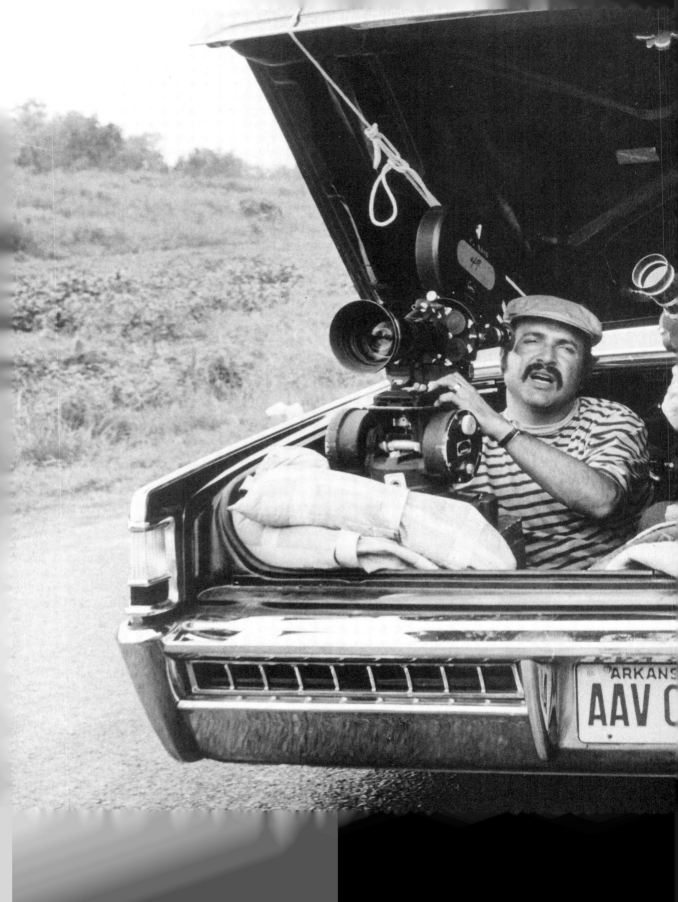

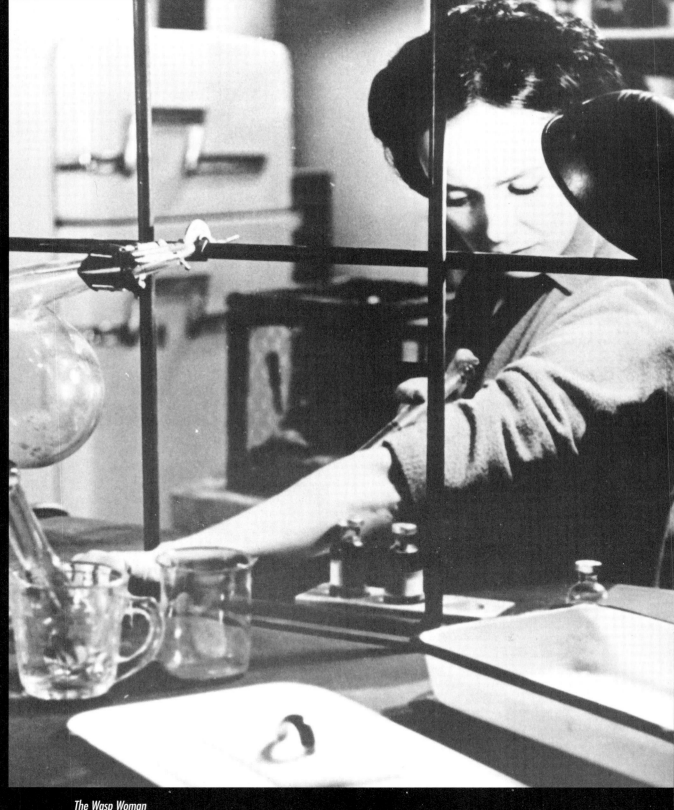

The Wasp Woman
1959 Susan Cabot regains her youth only to become a monster

THE WASP WOMAN

> **'Unexciting but exploitable horror film.'**

Having proved he could turn his hand very successfully to another type of film, Corman returned to his most popular genre, the fantastic film, with *The Wasp Woman* which was his first production for his own production/distribution company The Filmgroup.

He worked like a house afire and I like to work fast… whipping through that picture with Corman was a lot of fun: in fact, he did some pretty strange things.
Anthony Eisley

Backstory

Corman spent $50,000 on *The Wasp Woman* shot it in, as he recalls, five or six days at an understandably fast and furious pace. Eisley remembered: 'He would set up one camera angle on a particular setting that may appear in the picture five times. And then you would do all five scenes, changing your clothes between each scene. And then he'd set up the *other* camera angle, over your shoulder, and you'd do the five different scenes *again*, changing your clothes five times again!' Cabot found her role challenging: she was required to bring down men a foot taller than she was, and had to keep chocolate in her mouth which she could then extrude onto the necks of the victims she bit where on monochrome film it would hopefully pass for blood.

'What we did for Roger Corman – I mean, things that you could never do in a real studio but you did for this guy! Everything seemed unreal with him', said Cabot. '*The Wasp Woman* was totally isolated from a nor-

mal kind of feeling, and that was a wonderful growth experience for me; I think that was the most fun part I've ever had. To be able to go from a 40-year-old character to a 22-year-old one was a challenge. Then, to be a monster – one of the very few female beasties in movies – was great fun.'

Story

A cosmetics executive regains her youthful looks with a serum derived from wasp enzymes but unfortunate side-effects transform her into a killer wasp.

A more monstrous than terrifying addition to the 1950s cycle of giant bug movies with the courage of its own entertainingly lurid convictions. The poster proclaimed, 'A Beautiful Woman By Day – A Lusting Queen Wasp By Night' and showed a giant wasp with a woman's face wrapping its legs around a male victim. In the film, however, Cabot wore a patently fake wasp-face mask and kept her own body.

Reviews

'Unexciting but exploitable horror film. Film has interesting points and looks polished but it's pretty slow and not very frightening. It's exploitable, though … Daniel Haller makes the sets look smart and producer-director Roger Corman has them nicely peopled with probable characters who act fairly convincingly.'
Variety

'Most of the thrills in this horror story are provided by eerie music simulating the intense buzzing of wasps and the occasional wearing of an outsize wasp mask by the woman of the title. Apart from this, the atmosphere is mainly executive suite, with a laboratory of test tubes putting in an appearance now and then. The story is unfolded without much waste of time and the climax is quick and neat. A sprinkling of bloodshed completes the picture as average of the type with an appeal to the more easily pleased of science fiction fans.'
CEA Film Report

'A few steps above the trite trash of this period.'
Trumpet 4

'Not nearly as bad as we had expected... just a little more effort to co-ordinate the script and 'monster' would have resulted in a pair of superior science fiction pictures... (*Wasp*) (had a) 'fairly sophisticated story... Leo Gordon's script is smoothly urbane with nice surprising little touches here and there. Slim, intense, brunette Susan Cabot, who always impresses, does excellently nuanced work as the lady with the worries and the wasps.'
Los Angeles Times (seen in double bill with *Beast from Haunted Cave*)

'The earlier, more realistic scenes of this modest shocker, which is slow to get going, are pretty unlikely, while the latter bouts of fantasy are ludicrous rather than terrifying. Routine stuff, in fact, for determined enthusiasts only.'
Monthly Film Bulletin

CREDITS

The Wasp Woman (US 1959)
pc Filmgroup/Santa Clara
w Leo Gordon
ph Harry C Newman
ad Daniel Haller
mu Grant R Keats
p, d Roger Corman
st Kinta Zertuche
ed Carlo Lodato
m Fred Katz
73 mins.
Cast: Susan Cabot (Janice Starlin), Fred (Anthony) Eisley (Bill lane), Michael Mark (Eric Zinthrop), Barboura Morris (Mary Dennison), William Roerick (Arthur Cooper [Coop]), Frank Gerstle (Les Hellman), Bruno Ve Sota (Night Watchman), Roy Gordon (Max Thompson), Frank Wolff (Delivery Man), Carolyn Hughes (Jean Carson), Lynn Cartwright (Maureen Reardon), Lani Mars (Nurse Warren), Roger Corman (Emergency Doctor)

'In a snowy setting which gets monotonous, this war episode is dramatically half-hearted with little excitement; the action is confined to a few skirmishes with rifle fire and stabbings, padding with Nazi documentary cuts and a climax of the blowing-up of a bridge which is prolonged and does little to help the dullness of the poorly told exploit.'
CEA Film Report

'A crude war film which just about gets by when it sticks to action... the absence of perspective, depth and distance in the direction blunts the battle scenes, and in particular the climactic destruction of the bridge.'
Monthly Film Bulletin

CREDITS

Ski Troop Attack (US 1960)
pc Filmgroup   **p, d** Roger Corman
w Charles Griffith   **ph** Andy Costikyan
bw   **ed** Anthony Carras
m Fred Katz   63 mins.
Cast: Michael Forest (Lieutenant Factor), Frank Wolff (Potter), Wally Campo (Ed), Richard Sinatra (Herman), Sheila Carol (Lisa), Roger Corman (German soldier), Paul Rapp (Radio operator)

A BUCKET OF BLOOD

'Above average exploitation horror film with comedy elements.'

Corman then capitalised on the success of the blend of horror and gallows humour that had given *Not of this Earth* an entertaining impact over and above its genre parameters by making the three out-and-out black comedies that marked a major change in his output and helped made him 'respectable' in the eyes of the critics who were following (a long way behind, as usual) the audiences who had made his films profitable.

I believe A Bucket of Blood *is truly the cult film of all cult films. It ranks with some of the great classics of the silent era. Very, very few films are in every film museum in the world.* A Bucket of Blood *is.*
Dick Miller

Backstory

'The idea developed in a funny way,' Corman told me. 'Chuck Griffith the writer, who is a good friend of mine, and I had wanted to do a comedy-horror film. This was the original idea. And I had nothing more in mind than that.

'So Chuck and I went out to dinner on Sunset Strip, and then we started drifting from coffee house to coffee house on the strip, talking about ideas, developing them, throwing one out after another, and we ended up in the early morning at Chez Paulette where one of the waitresses came over and sat with us as they were closing up.

'It was Sally Kellerman whom we knew as a good young actress and who wasn't working, so was working as a waitress. Sally sat with us at the table and helped us and she threw up some ideas and by the end of the evening we had the story line.'

Corman made the film for $50,000 in five days (and beat his previous shooting record by a day). 'I've played Walter [Paisley] five times now, I think,' said Miller. 'I've lost count. There was *A Bucket of Blood, Hollywood Boulevard* and *The Howling*. In *Twilight Zone – The Movie* there's a sign in the back of the restaurant that says "Walter Paisley, Proprietor". I played a night watchman in Alan Arkush's film, *Heartbeeps* and I am wearing a name tag that says Walter Paisley. I don't remember if it said the whole name or just Paisley.' Miller also reprised Paisley in *Chopping Mall* (1986) and in the 1995 television remake of *Bucket of Blood*.

Julian Burton, excellent as the pompous beatnik poet, makes a serendipitous fashion statement when he turns up at an art exhibition wearing sandals with evening dress although this was actually because he was unable to put on his shoes because his feet were swollen.

AIP promoted *A Bucket of Blood* as a comedy with the tag line 'You'll be *sick, sick, sick* – from LAUGH-ING!' and offered exhibitors useful promotional ideas.

'The first thing that should be set up in your lobby is a giant bucket that is tipped to the side and has the appearance of red fluid dripping. This can be done with some art or possibly just filling the bucket with red dye.

Paths of red drippings should lead from various strategic points of the city to your theatre.

Make some sort of arrangement with your local Red Cross to have a tie-in with *A Bucket of Blood*, whereby they would get enough volunteers to fill many buckets. This could even be tied in with your local newspapers.

Feature a special 'Blood Drink', and for those patrons who might have thin blood, give them a red candy pill, representing a blood builder and energy pill for witnessing *A Bucket of Blood*.

Have contests such as, 'How many *Buckets of Blood* would a human be able to fill?'. Or, 'How many different blood types are there?'

Story

A browbeaten waiter at a coffee bar, who is hailed as a sculptor of genius by beatnik customers after he encases the corpse of a dead cat in clay, turns to murder to create new 'masterpieces'.

Corman wittily blends black humour, horror and a cruelly accurate satire of the overweening pretensions of the then much-admired Beatnik poets, drawing a highly effective performance from his 'repertory regular' Miller as the archetypal nerd-as-hero-villain Walter Paisley in a clever riff on *The Mystery of the Wax Museum* and *House of Wax* that has deservedly become a cult classic.

Reviews

'Above average exploitation horror film with comedy elements: aimed at youth market. A 66-minute joke compounded of beatniks and gore. It's too comic to be a typical horror film and the horror is too explicit for it to be a comedy, but for the youth market at which it's aimed, the feature looks like a winner... Dick Miller's ability to sustain a sense of poignancy while acting conceited and committing atrocities is responsible in large part for the picture's appeal. With other actors – notably Barboura Morris, Anthony Carbone and Julian Burton – producer-director Roger Corman has made equally happy choices. Corman has expertly captured the expresso house atmosphere and peopled it with accurate characters, the real-life counterparts of whom should wince... it's perhaps idle to speculate on what Corman might have come up with if he had more time and money for the film and had he not been bound by the necessity of providing the bucket of blood promised in the title (a man's head is severed with a circular saw and ichor drips into a bucket from a corpse's hiding place in the rafters – all pretty sickening). The film will sell as is. But it might have been a very satisfying satire.'
Variety

'This horror film certainly attempts to get out of the routine rut. Its macabre moments are effective though not too grisly, and the killings, though well led up to, are not fully shown. The difficult central role of the crushed timid underdog menial is cleverly played by Dick Miller. Parts of the film, notably the earlier scenes, are a glorious satire on jargon-spouting beatniks and phoney artists, led by a mystic poet who recites to jazz, but this aspect of the picture might strike many audiences as either silly or bewildering, though others might find it rather amusing. In other respects, there is sufficient horror hokum to entertain the fans.'
CEA Film Report

'Wild, unusual, macabre Corman drama... Offbeat, not always successful, but plenty of atmosphere and some fair satire. Worthwhile. Well acted by Richard Miller, Barboura Morris, Anthony Carbone.'
Castle of Frankenstein

'Though the horror ultimately becomes rather too explicit, this macabre satire on beatniks and teenage horror films has some particularly adroit dialogue and tragi-comic situations. Dick Miller gives a performance of sustained poignancy as the half-wit hero, production values are modest but adequate, the handling most efficient; and under these circumstances it would perhaps be unfair to suggest that it really requires a Buñuel to get away with this kind of off-beat experiment.'
Monthly Film Bulletin

CREDITS ⟩⟩⟩⟩⟩⟩⟩⟩⟩⟩⟩⟩⟩

A Bucket of Blood (US 1959)
pc AIP. A James H Nicholson and Sam Arkoff production
p, d Roger Corman   **w** Charles B Griffith
ph Jack Marquette   **bw**
ed Anthony Carras   **ad** Dan Haller
m Fred Katz   **saxophone solo** Paul Horn
mu Bob Mark   66 mins.
Cast: Dick Miller (Walter Paisley), Barboura Morris (Carla), Antony Carbone (Leonard), Julian Burton (Maxwell H Brock), Ed Nelson (Art Lacroix), John Brinkley (Will), John Shaner (Oscar), Judy Bamber (Alice), Myrtle Domerel (Mrs Surchart), Burt Convy (Lou Raby), Jhean Burton (Naolia)

CREATURE FROM THE HAUNTED SEA

'Unanticipated entertainment.'

Corman enjoyed the two weeks he had spent shooting *The Last Woman on Earth* and decided to stay on and make another film, *Creature from the Haunted Sea*.

There are no good guys who destroy the monster. The monster wins.
Roger Corman

Backstory

Corman began filming *Creature from the Haunted Sea* on a Monday with the cast of *The Last Woman on Earth* (Carbone, Jones-Moreland and Wain/Towne) which he had completed the previous Saturday. He gave Griffith a week to write the script and agreed to play a minor part to save paying an actor. Griffith wrote the role of Happy Jack Monahan for Corman, making him the most complex character in the film. Corman sensibly gave the part to actor/boom operator Bobby Beam who also doubled inside the monster which was created by Beech Dickerson (who had been part of the crab monster team in *Attack of the Crab Monsters*) for just $150 using tennis balls, ping-pong balls, with pipe cleaners for claws and an oilskin cloth to make it look slimy.

Story

A gangster using his boat to help loyalists escape with a fortune in gold from a revolution-ridden Caribbean island plans to kill them, steal the gold and blame the deaths on a legendary sea monster – unfortunately, a real monster turns up and starts doing his dirty work for him.

Brisk, agreeably zany if somewhat threadbare horror-comedy with the emphasis on the latter and an appropriately ludicrous monster.

Reviews

'A most engaging spoof on the horror element... some engaging thespians who cavort with spiritedness... unanticipated entertainment... if there exists a 'New Wave' in the US-based film industry, it must be Corman, who ranks as chief of state.'
Boxoffice

(Corman's) 'distinctive, decisive flair'.
Motion Picture Herald

CREDITS ▶▶▶▶▶▶▶▶▶▶▶▶

Creature from the Haunted Sea (US 1960)
pc Filmgroup
d pre-title sequence Monte Hellman
w Charles B Griffith
bw
monster construction Beech Dickerson, Robert Bean
m Fred Katz
60 mins.
p, d, add **w** Roger Corman
assoc p Charles Hannawalt
ph Jacques Marquette
ed Angela Scellars

mu Brooke Wilkerson

Cast: Antony Carbone (Renzo), Betsy Jones-Moreland (Mary-Belle), Edward Wain aka Robert Towne (Sparks Moran), Edmundo Rivera Alvarez (Colonel Tostada), Robert Bean (Happy Jack Monahan), Sonya Noemi Gonzalez (Mango Perez), Beech Dickerson (Pete Peterson Jr), Elisio Lopez, Binaquita Rome

Part 3

THE HOUSE THAT POE BUILT

Corman, as Terence Fisher had done when, in 1956, he made *The Curse of Frankenstein* and *Dracula/Horror of Dracula* for Britain's Hammer Films, opened up a highly profitable and critically respectable new vein of horror when he segued from the fast and furious world of B feature films into the literally wider CinemaScope era of his classic Freud-influenced Edgar Allan Poe adaptations that began in 1960 with *House of Usher*.

THE FALL OF THE HOUSE OF USHER

> '...striking, elaboration on Poe's short story.'

I like the Poe films. As a matter of fact, they are an example of low-budget film-making. They were all shot on three-week schedules – 15 days – for all of them. Except for the last two, which we shot in England which were five-week schedules – 25 days – The Tomb of Ligeia *and* The Masque of the Red Death.
Roger Corman

Backstory

'I never started out to do a series on Edgar Allen Poe. I simply wanted to do *The Fall of the House of Usher* which was a big step forward for AIP because they wanted me to do two ten-day black and white horror films. This was the style Jim Nicholson and I had sort of put together, that you had two low budget pictures. There wasn't an A picture and a B picture; they were 50/50 in the ads and you could sell them against a major studio's one picture. I did it for AIP and I did it for Allied Artists a number of times. Then AIP had asked me to do two more of them – two more ten-day black and white horror pictures for them.

'I talked to Jim and I said, "I think this was a great idea but we have done it too often." I also had my own ulterior motives. "I think we would be better off to shoot a picture in colour. Let me have 15 days and let's try for one feature." And he asked me what I wanted to do. I had always loved *The Fall of the House of Usher*.

'I had a meeting with Jim and then a second meeting with Jim and Sam Arkoff. Sam was somewhat opposed to it because there was no monster. And I said "The house *is* the monster!" and he said okay. They agreed. It was a gamble on their part. I felt the gamble would be successful. I didn't know that it would be *so* successful. As it was, they asked me to do one after the other and finally I stopped. They wanted me to continue but I just said that I had done enough of them,' Corman told me.

Corman's choice of Vincent Price as his leading man got the series off to a flying start. 'Price was a well-educated, highly cultured man,' recalled Price in 1995. 'I cast him in our first film together, *The Fall of the House of Usher*, because the character of Roderick Usher was very close to his own persona: handsome, educated, cultured and sensitive. In the Edgar Allan Poe story, Roderick Usher is a gentle, aristocratic man who progressively descends into madness. My feeling was that the audience should be frightened of this character, but not in conscious reaction to his sinister features or brute strength. Instead, I envisioned a refined, attractive man whose intelligent but tormented mind operates in realms far beyond the minds of others, and who therefore inspires a deeper fear. In Vincent I found exactly the man I was looking for... In every case he was a valued contributor to the creative process.

In *The Fall of the House of Usher*, he was asked to speak the line, 'The house lives. The house breathes.' He came to me and asked in great bewilderment, 'What does that mean?' "It means", I replied, "That we are

AMERICAN INTERNATIONAL presents

EDGAR ALLAN POE'S

classic tale of THE UNGODLY..THE EVIL

HOUSE OF USHER

in CinemaScope and COLOR   starring VINCENT PRICE

"I heard her first
feeble movements
in the coffin...
we had put her
living in the tomb!"
—Poe

able to make this picture." Once this was explained to him, Vincent said, "I understand totally." He went on to deliver the line with a subtle intensity that became for me one of the high points of the entire film.'

Price, who was paid $50,000 out of the budget of some $270,000 (the largest sum of money AIP had ever allocated to the production of a single film), later stated: 'I still think almost the best of all of them was *House of Usher*. I loved that. I loved the white-haired character I was playing because he is the most sensitive of all Poe's hero's – he's hypersensitive.'

'There was only one time that I ever saw Vincent Price angry', recalled screenwriter Richard Matheson. 'Mark Damon comes in, and he's about to strike Price with an axe. He flings the axe down, and it bounces right off Price's shin. Price uttered the only profanity I ever heard him say, left the stage and walked around the whole thing. And when he came back, he was himself again.'
Richard Matheson

House of Usher also marked the first of Corman's seminal collaborations with writer Richard Matheson. 'Except for maybe some of the short Poe stories I adapted for *Tales of Terror*, *House of Usher* probably came closest to the original. I tried to stay close, but even at that I added a romance to it', Matheson later recalled.

Corman was particularly well served by art director Daniel Haller who bought stock sets and scenery for some $25,000 from Universal and used them to create a surprisingly (for AIP) expensive-looking production on sound stages at the old Chaplin studio, which Floyd Crosby's atmospheric cinematography then made look even more sumptuous. Serendipity, too, played a part in its success.

At the opening of the picture, Mark Damon rides towards the eponymous mansion through a bleak, blackened wilderness of charred trees, ash and fog. Corman added the fog when he filmed the sequence in the aftermath of a forest fire that had fortuitously burned out part of the Hollywood Hills at the start of production. The spectacular destruction of the House of Usher at the climax was equally fortuitous. Corman persuaded the owner of a derelict old barn not to have it demolished by developers but instead to allow him to burn it down at night. He covered the conflagration with two

cameras, creating a vivid sequence of destruction that was to become something of a Corman trademark in the tradition of the pitchfork brandishing villagers who usually brought Universal's Thirties and Forties monster movies to a close.

'We had good stock footage, we used it and then we added to it with each picture because I would have the fire for that particular film. I'd have what I'd shot for *that* film plus what I could add from the others,' Corman told me. 'For instance, in *The Terror*, the house is destroyed by a flood, and it was destroyed by a flood only because I was tired of burning the house down and I thought what could I do other than burn the house down. So I went to the exact opposite – I went from fire to water.'

Corman completed the film in 15 days.

'It was one of those rare films where we had both the critical acclaim and the box office success, so we could kind of sit back and see it coming from all directions.'
Roger Corman

House of Usher earned in excess of $1 million.

'A not altogether faithful, but nevertheless striking, elaboration on Poe's short story. Should appeal to wide range of tastes, and score widely at the b.o.'

Story
When Philip Winthrop comes to claim his fiancée Madeline Usher, her sinister brother Roderick refuses to allow them to marry because of a family curse: Madeline apparently dies but has actually been buried alive and returns from the grave to bring about the end of the House of Usher.

Corman creates a highly effective atmosphere of mounting unease reinforced by fluid camerawork and heightened use of colour and wide screen and Price is commanding as the tortured, white-haired Roderick Usher. Corman also establishes the cobwebbed, echoing corridors and vaults to which he would return to vivid dramatic effect in subsequent Poe pictures and also wittily to underline comedy in *The Raven*.

Reviews
'A not altogether faithful, but nevertheless striking, elaboration on Poe's short story. Should appeal to a wide

THE INTRUDER

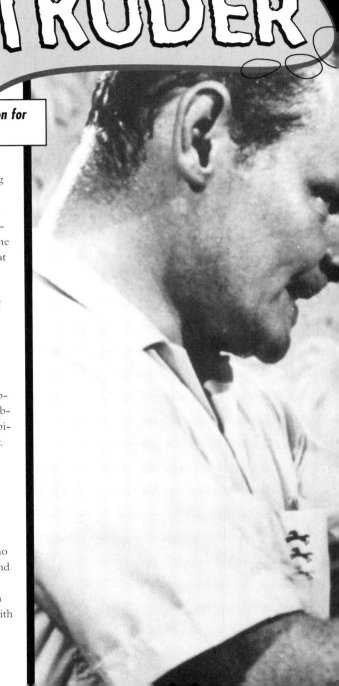

'Significant stride in timely sociological direction for US filmdom.'

Corman followed *The Pit and the Pendulum* by stepping both out of character as a maker of low-budget exploitation movies and out of genre and exposing his political and social beliefs with a passionate and powerful attack on racism that rightly earned him some of the best reviews. It was, ironically, also his first film to fail at the box-office.

I think it was on a subject that at that time the public didn't want to see. I made a film they didn't want to see.
Roger Corman

Backstory

The article *Intruder in the South* which described the attempts of Northern rabble-rouser John Kasper to sabotage school integration in Clinton, Tennessee, was published in *Look* magazine in 1957 and served as the inspiration for Charles Beaumont's 1958 novel *The Intruder*. Beaumont adapted his novel for the screen and also appeared in front of the camera as school principal Harley Paton.

Corman intended to make no concessions to Southern segregationists and, moreover, to shoot *The Intruder* entirely on location: unsurprisingly, he was unable to raise finance from major film companies who ran scared from the potential for controversy. In the end Corman and his brother Gene co-financed the film with Pathé laboratories (who later became involved in Corman's abortive attempt to break away from AIP with *The Premature Burial*) topping up the budget. 'The Intruder was a film that Roger and I always wanted to make, and it involved some of our basic precepts,' said Gene Corman.

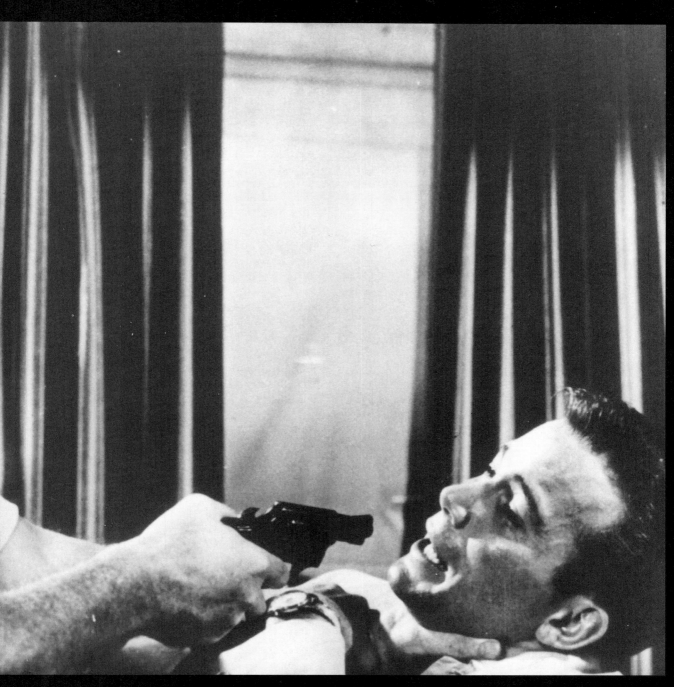

The Intruder
William Shatner (right) in his first starring role and in Corman's first box-office flop

the Kentucky-Illinois border. Corman used leads from Los Angeles and cast locals in key roles in order to achieve authenticity: Missouri honours student Charles Barnes portrayed the African-American youth who leads his classmates to school in the face of fierce opposition, a genuine minister agreed to 'die' in the church explosion and a real-life high school teacher played a mob victim.

The Intruder was filmed in just three weeks with only the director and William Shatner, in his first starring role, in possession of complete copies of the screenplay, with Corman deliberately diluting controversial (for the South) dialogue in order not to inflame local sensitivities. Even so, the unit came under constant pressure from the law and the locals and there were overt threats, particularly when it came to the staging of the major crowd scenes.

Said Shatner: 'We were surrounded by some very emotional people down there. Our lives were threatened...We shot a white supremacy parade through the black part of town and a cross-burning scene at night and while this was being shot someone watching in the crowd was shot. The whites thought we were with the blacks and they hated us. It was murder. Those three weeks seemed interminable.'

Noted writer William F Nolan who, like Beaumont, had a cameo role, 'Several explosive scenes were slated to take place on the playground outside the A J Webb school in East Prairie and Corman had obtained permission to occupy the area for three full days in order to frame the climax of the story... After two days of shooting we were paid a visit by the East Prairie police, warning us of possible harassment'. Corman's permit to film was abruptly cancelled and he was told he was no longer welcome in East Prairie. He managed to film his establishing shots but the sequence had to be completed at other playgrounds, including one in Charlston.

'It was greeted with incredible reviews, the best reviews I think I have ever had,' Corman told me. 'It opened in New York to incredibly good reviews from the *New York Herald Tribune*. I still have it memorised: "This motion picture is a major credit to the entire American film industry." And it just got good review after good review after good review and won a couple of film festivals. It was indeed the first film I ever made that lost money. I think it was partially the distribution in that it didn't

come from a distinguished company and wasn't presented to the public the way I ended up in the Seventies when I was distributing Bergman and Fellini and Kurosawa and so forth. But also two things. One, they didn't want to deal with that subject and second, I may have been too earnest in stating too clearly what my film was about. After that I rethought what I was doing and I went back to a genre-type of film-making in which, on the surface, I would deliberately do a gangster film, the horror film, the science fiction film and if I had something to say, I would say it *sub-textually* so the text would be the gangster film, the sub-text would be my thoughts about gangsters and how they fit in society – but it would still be a gangster film.'

'In retrospect,' said Corman in 1991, 'I think it became a little bit more of a "message film" than it should have. What I've tried to do since is to make pictures that on the surface are more of an entertainment, and any themes or ideas I have I try to keep beneath the surface.'

Story

A rabble-rousing white supremacist comes to a small Southern town on the eve of racial integration in the local school, insinuates himself into the community and inflames racial tensions that lead to the bombing of a church and a near lynching.

Corman proved himself a crusading, ahead-of-his-time and deeply committed filmmaker: the honesty and very real anger that pervades the proceedings makes up for some over-schematic plotting and some forays into out-and-out melodrama, the character drawing is surprisingly three-dimensional, the professional (and many of the amateur) players acquit themselves with credit and only the rather too-simplistic resolution that leads to the dispersal of the would-be lynch mob fails to convince.

Reviews

'Resourcefully produced indie drama. Significant stride in timely sociological direction for US filmdom, but will have to be marketed with care and taste to stimulate deserved b.o. reaction... comes to grips with a controversial contemporary issue – integration, and those who would defy the law of the land – in an adult, intelligent and arresting manner. Limited funds have not

deterred these two filmmakers (Roger and Gene) from tackling this significant subject boldly, honestly and uncompromisingly. The film, a Pathé America release, is a credit to an industry that has been charged, and not without cause, of playing it safe by avoiding ticklish, pertinent, up-to-date sociological matters in view of commercial realities. While *The Intruder* is obviously not going to cause any box-office stampede, it can, if sold as resourcefully as it was produced, emerge a profitable commercial enterprise as well as an important, worthwhile artistic effort and a boost to the prestige of US filmdom in more influential, discriminating circles here and abroad. The picture is not without one or two major story flaws, but these shortcomings are overridden by its innate overall significance. The main thing is that this is a provocative, timely matter of importance and concern to all Americans and this should be emphasized. The film should not be cheapened in the selling by playing up its sexual or psychological ramifications... This film is a major credit to the Cormans (producer-director Roger and exec producer Gene), scenarist Beaumont, cameraman Taylor Byars, editor Ronald Sinclair and composer Herman Stein, as well as others responsible for its execution. It is a sign of a new maturity on the part of the US motion picture industry. It must not be allowed to expire of malnutrition in its embryo stage.'
Variety

'A sombre but arresting and often suspenseful story, boldly told on a timely and controversial theme, this well-produced and compellingly acted picture grips the attention from the start and holds it throughout the tense action. Its appeal should be fairly general among filmgoers who like strong, serious drama, for it should interest both popular and good-class audiences.'
CEA Film Report

'Corman's crusading spirit and enterprise have paid off.'
Monthly Film Bulletin

'Some highly explosive material is handled crudely and a bit too clumsily for either conviction or comfort in *The Intruder*, an angry little film turned out by Roger and Gene Corman... But this must be said for *The Intruder*, it does break fertile ground in the area of integration that has not yet been opened on the screen. And it does so with obvious good intentions and a great deal of raw, arresting power in many of its individual details and in the aspects of several characters... it marks the intrusion of an area that begs to be further explored by dramatists and cinematists with talent. Call it an enterprising try.'
The New York Times

'Corman... (has) abandoned his vampires, his monsters from the ocean floor, his drag strip girls, and his Apache women to take a hard look at the American scene, and at a monster inspired by real life: John Kasper, the arch segregationalist whose rabble-rousing activities made headlines in 1957... much of the strength of the film comes from the fact that it was shot on location, with townspeople all too willingly playing themselves on screen... the real people and the real settings serve as a constant reminder that this is not a charade.'
The Saturday Review

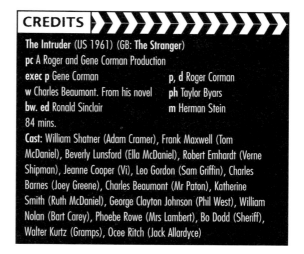

CREDITS

The Intruder (US 1961) (GB: **The Stranger**)
pc A Roger and Gene Corman Production
exec p Gene Corman   **p, d** Roger Corman
w Charles Beaumont. From his novel   **ph** Taylor Byars
bw. ed Ronald Sinclair   **m** Herman Stein
84 mins.
Cast: William Shatner (Adam Cramer), Frank Maxwell (Tom McDaniel), Beverly Lunsford (Ella McDaniel), Robert Emhardt (Verne Shipman), Jeanne Cooper (Vi), Leo Gordon (Sam Griffin), Charles Barnes (Joey Greene), Charles Beaumont (Mr Paton), Katherine Smith (Ruth McDaniel), George Clayton Johnson (Phil West), William Nolan (Bart Carey), Phoebe Rowe (Mrs Lambert), Bo Dodd (Sheriff), Walter Kurtz (Gramps), Ocee Ritch (Jack Allardyce)

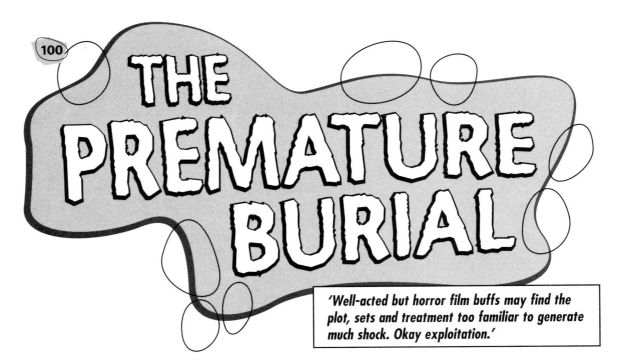

THE PREMATURE BURIAL

'Well-acted but horror film buffs may find the plot, sets and treatment too familiar to generate much shock. Okay exploitation.'

After the critical success and commercial failure of *The Intruder*, Corman profitably returned to Poe and Gothic horror with *The Premature Burial*.

That's one of my favourites. There was a mood to it, a strangeness and a mood.
Hazel Court

Backstory

Corman was tired of flipping a coin with Samuel Z Arkoff as a cavalier way of settling their disputes over profit shares on previous pictures and decided to go with Pathé Laboratories who had put some money into *The Intruder* and were keen to become involved in film production. Corman cast Ray Milland. 'I went with Ray', he claimed, 'because I thought he was very good and right for the role but also Vincent had in his contract with AIP that he couldn't do a horror film for anybody but AIP. They wanted to make him *their* star so since the picture started out not being AIP – that's why I went with Ray.'

Then Arkoff and Nicholson turned up on the set of *The Premature Burial*. 'Well, at first I was surprised and didn't like it', Corman told me. 'Then I thought it was funny because they came to the set on the morning of the first day of shooting and they came in to wish me well. I thought that was nice of them.

'Then Sam who was a funny guy at times said, "Roger, we are happy to become partners again," and I said, "What do you mean?" and he said, "We have made

a deal with Pathé. We have bought 'em up; we are all working together again." For a moment I was startled, but within a minute, within a few seconds actually, I laughed.'

Charles Beaumont and Ray Russell had to elaborate on the Poe original in order to create a holding storyline and emphasised Poe's fear of being buried alive to considerable suspenseful effect while at the same time injecting a modicum of humour which Corman felt worked well with horror. 'There's a very fine line between horror and humour. On *The Premature Burial* I did some reading, and talked with psychologists, one who had written a book called *Beyond Laughter*. In it, he discussed the psychological origins of laughter and terror, which he felt were two sides of the same coin,' noted Corman

Hammer horror star Hazel Court made her first (of two) Hollywood pictures with Corman before returning to England to star in his Poe classic *The Masque of the Red Death* in 1964. 'They actually did bury me!' Court recalled in a *Fangoria* interview. 'On rehearsals I had a straw in my mouth, and in covering me up, they didn't cover the top of the straw. But on the actual take I had to hold my breath for a minute – a full 60 seconds – covered up with cork. It was *horrible*!'

Story

A Victorian who suffers from catalepsy has a morbid terror of being buried alive and when his worst fears are realised he returns from the grave with homicide on his mind.

The Premature Burial
1962 Roger Corman on the set

PARDON FILMS
PRÉSENTE - STELT VOOR
AVEC - MET
HAZEL COURT
RICHARD NEY · HEATHER ANGEL
EASTMANCOLOR
SCOPE
LEVEND
BEGRAVEN
PROD: A.I.P.
IMPRIME EN BELGIQUE

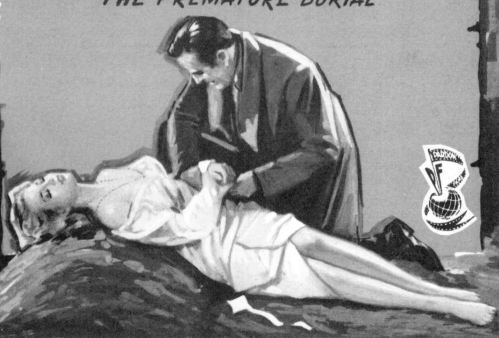

RAY MILLAND

DANS UNE ŒUVRE DE • NAAR EEN WERK VAN

EDGAR ALLAN POE

ENTERRÉ VIVANT

"THE PREMATURE BURIAL"

Éditeur Responsable : Maurice PANNEELS - 26, Rue Martin Pfeiffer, Bruxelles - Tél. 26.10.81

Visually Corman is on top form: he uses his by now 'traditional' Gothic trappings of mists and moody mansions effectively to create a telling atmosphere of claustrophobia, and excellent sound design heightens the suspense, but the screenplay contains too many familiar elements from his previous Poe pictures and Milland, while good, lacks the larger-than-life dimension that Price brought to his roles.

Reviews

'Well-acted but horror film buffs may find the plot, sets and treatment too familiar to generate much shock. Okay exploitation. Producer-director Roger Corman seems to have run a bit thin in imagination on this third trip to the same literary well. Not only is the plotting in *Premature Burial* discouragingly predictable, but its gloomy and cavernous interior setting is peculiarly similar to those in the first two. By this time many film fans (and at least one reviewer) are as familiar with Corman's downstairs dungeon as they are with their own basement hobbyshops. The picture obviously has hefty exploitation potential via its title and Poe's rep. However, it's unlikely that its appeal will reach beyond the circle of the horror buffs to attract those patrons who were so delighted by ghoulish fustian of the *Usher* and *Pit*. Ironically, it may be that the extremely competent cast, headed by Ray Milland, plays too honestly in situations which require a certain amount of unrestrained flamboyance... screenplay, though short on the kind of plot surprises which create suspense and interest, is cleanly dialogued with a minimum of verbal clichés. And Floyd Crosby's camerawork (in colour and Panavision) is as effective as ever, although he and Corman might try eschewing those blue-and-purple dream sequences next time out.'
Variety

'While this frank horror yarn is static, slack and starchily written, it does have the same visual attributes as last season's *The Pit and the Pendulum*: compelling music, rich colour décor and eerie atmosphere. This time, however, the fusion isn't so successful in sustaining the suspense.'
The New York Times

'Poe's classic story has been padded out with plenty of swirling mist, thunderstorms, a creepy family vault, colour dream tricks and a 'gimmick' which consists of blacking out the screen entirely to the sound of heartbeats. Some of the dialogue and situations may raise an unintentional laugh or two, but the cast enter with gusto into the bogey-bogey thrills of the old-fashioned kind of 'chiller' – and the masses will do the same.'
CEA Film Report

'Corman's serviceable horror tale, loosely based on Poe... A few good spots.'
Castle of Frankenstein

'The outlandish horror of Poe's story is never really caught, and Corman obtains most of his effects from rude shock-cuts rather than from intelligent exploitation of the situations and settings.'
Monthly Film Bulletin

'Mr Corman's production group, the only outfit in Hollywood with a spider under long-term contact, has made several handsome horror pictures in the past. *The Premature Burial* is no less attractively designed or tastefully coloured.'
The New York Herald Tribune

CREDITS ❯❯❯❯❯❯❯❯❯❯❯❯❯❯❯

The Premature Burial (US 1962)
pc Santa Clara   **exec p** Gene Corman
p, d Roger Corman   **w** Charles Beaumont, Ray Russell
Suggested by the story Tale of Illusion by Edgar Allan Poe
ph Floyd Crosby   **colour.** Panavision
ed Ronald Sinclair   **ad** Daniel Haller
cost Marjorie Corso   **m** Ronald Stein
81 mins.
Cast: Ray Milland (Guy Carrell), Hazel Court (Emily Gault), Richard Ney (Miles Archer), Heather Angel (Kate Carrell), Alan Napier (Dr Gideon Gault), John Dierkes (Sweeney), Richard (Dick) Miller (Mole), Brendan Dillon (Minister)

TALES OF TERROR

'Promising bet in the goose-bump market.'

Corman revived the portmanteau format of several short films that had been successfully used in the classic 1945 British shocker *Dead of Night* for his next Poe adaptation, *Tales of Terror*. As he had done in *The Premature Burial*, he once again injected humour into the horrific proceedings in the hilarious central story *The Black Cat* which remains the most memorable of the three tales.

My theories about comedy are that comedy is serious and that the actors or, should I put it another way, the characters, must never be aware that they are funny.
Roger Corman

Backstory

The casting was felicitous, co-starring Poe regular Vincent Price with Peter Lorre in *The Black Cat* and with Basil Rathbone in *The Facts in the Case of M Valdemar*, leaving Price to carry *Morella*. Screenwriter Richard Matheson was not pleased, telling *Fangoria*, 'I must sound like an egomaniac, but once again I thought that was a good script. On that first segment [*Morella*], the casting really bugged me. I always refer to that first segment as 'Shirley Temple in the Haunted House'. In my script, it was a really great character relationship between the two of them: Vincent Price was up to it, and I was visualising someone like Nina Foch playing the dying daughter. But this girl they got was terrible, and they also cut a lot out of it, so it just didn't work.' In fact, it did, although the fiery climax was by now becoming something of a Corman cliché.

'I worked well with Basil,' said Corman. 'He was very well prepared. He would come in knowing his lines to the letter, with an interpretation, we would discuss the part a little bit, and he required the minimum of direction, as did Vincent.'

Given the dialogue-heavy nature of the episode (and of *Morella*), Corman cleverly created visual interest by moving both camera and the actors. *The Black Cat* gave Corman the very well-taken opportunity to demonstrate that he could translate his theories about comedy into film fact. Not all critics reacted favourably. Filmgoers, on the other hand, did. 'Peter Lorre loved the challenge of working with the works of Edgar Allan Poe', said Corman. 'He was a very fine actor and a very serious actor. I think he was one of the most creative men I've ever met and he understood as much as anybody in today's world can... Peter was a natural comic.'

Story: Morella

For 26 years a recluse guards the mummified corpse of his wife who died in childbirth, until her spirit possesses their daughter with terrible consequences.

The Black Cat

A henpecked husband who finally rebels and walls up his wife and her lover unfortunately immures a telltale crying cat with them.

The Facts in the Case of M Valdemar

The unscrupulous mesmerist who hypnotises a dying man at the point of death and leaves him in living limbo is frightened to death when his victim awakes and dissolves into slime.

Tales of Terror: *Morella, The Black Cat and The Facts in the Case of M Valdemar*
Vincent Price takes on a role in all three

There are occasions in the gloomy but atmospheric and eerie mansion-bound *Morella* when Corman teeters dangerously close to self-parody and *The Facts in the Case of M Valdemar* suffers from less than ideal make-up effects when Price dissolves on camera but both episodes are strong and powerfully acted by Price and Rathbone. *The Black Cat*, which also combines elements of Poe's *The Cask of Amontillado*, is witty, winning and perfectly played by Price and Lorre whose larger-than-life performances and, in the case of the latter, apparent ad-libbing, are exactly right for the material.

Reviews

'Promising bet in the goose-bump market. The three tales make a heavy dose, even for the thrill-prone teenage set. It's to the credit of producer-director Roger Corman that the first two, *Morella* and *The Black Cat*, trip through the horror hoops in a mad grace going strictly beyond fan appeal. Corman and scenarist Richard Matheson do get bogged down in the long-winded latter story... It's only the final scene in *Valdemar* which is a shocker – and a real ugly one at that. Whether audiences will have been rendered limp by the Poe cycle is anybody's guess. Producer Corman, though, plays his latest entry for all it's worth... the best realised nightmare and the shortest of the trio is *Morella*... this short piece is played for its nightmarish terror and it clicks, hitting hidden human recesses. Simulating a woman's face after 20-odd years of death is a matter of taste. This reviewer found it repulsive. *The Black Cat* ... is too long, but as a mad caper it has its moments... (*Valdemar*)... weakest.'
Variety

'...contains the familiar ingredients of an old eerie house, corpses coming to life and a fire climax, but it is well done and carries plenty of atmosphere. The first and last stories are 'spine-chillers' but the second (splendidly put over by Peter Lorre) features many touches of humour and some distorted photography to balance its finally gruesome tale... Effectively acted and presented, it makes good horror entertainment for the fans.'
CEA Film Report

'Aficionados of the weird, the strange, or what Poe called the 'grotesque' and 'arabesque' can troop, I think with good heart, to see *Tales of Terror*.'
New York Herald-Tribune

'By and large, Roger Corman's Poe adaptations maintain the highest standard in their field since Val Lewton's low-budget horror films of the Forties. Their basic material is respectable and – though never too literally – respected; the character acting is full-blooded and professional; sets, costumes and Richard Matheson's dialogue all have a consistently mock-Gothic flavour. Though still not rivalling Lewton's product, the three stories which make up *Tales of Terror* reveal these qualities at their best, with the added advantage that for once there is no sense of the material being stretched too thin.'
Monthly Film Bulletin

'Lavish but only intermittently successful.'
Castle of Frankenstein

CREDITS ▶▶▶▶▶▶▶▶▶▶▶▶▶

Tales of Terror (US 1962)
pc Alta Vista/AIP   **exec p** James H Nicholson, Samuel Z Arkoff
p, d Roger Corman   **w** Richard Matheson
From the stories Morella, The Black Cat, The Cask of Amontillado and The Facts in the Case of M Valdemar by Edgar Allan Poe
ph Floyd Crosby   **colour**
ed Anthony Carras   **ad** Daniel Haller
cost Marjorie Corso   **sfx** Pat Dinga
m Les Baxter   120 mins.
Cast: Morella Vincent Price (Locke), Maggie Pierce (Lenora), Leona Gage (Morella), Ed Cobb (Driver)
The Black Cat
Peter Lorre (Montresor), Vincent Price (Fortunato), Joyce Jameson (Annabel), Lennie Weinrib, John Hackett (Policemen), Wally Campo (Bartender), Alan Dewit (Chairman)
The Facts in the Case of M Valdemar
Vincent Price (M Valdemar), Basil Rathbone (Mr Carmichael), Debra Paget (Helene), David Frankham (Dr Eliot James), Scotty Brown (Servant)

American International

MUEL Z. ARKOFF   MUSIQUE: LES BAXTER
ICHARD MATHESON

LVERHALEN

EDICOLOR   Bruxelles   Tél. : 54.78.71

TOWER OF LONDON

ADMIRAL PICTURES, INC. presents
VINCENT PRICE
in " **TOWER OF LONDON** " ⊗
co-starring
MICHAEL PATE • JOAN FREEMAN • ROBERT BROWN

Tower of London
1962 Vincent Price as the Duke of Gloucester and the doomed young princes

Corman followed *Tales of Terror* with a low-budget exercise in ersatz Poe for Independent producer Edward Small.

Every trick of dastardy I ever learned,' Vincent says, 'was preparation for my role in Tower of London. *Then we added some new, diabolic devices to fill our Richard's character as one of the ten meanest men in the world.*
Tower of London pressbook

Backstory

Small was looking for an opportunity to cash in on the market for Poe chillers that Corman had created. Corman duly obliged but, believing Price had made quite enough forays into Poe, he turned to the Bard to provide a similarly Gothic vehicle for Vincent Price who had played the Duke of Clarence in Rowland V Lee's otherwise almost entirely dissimilar 1939 *Tower of London*.

Corman brought the film in around 15 days on a budget of under $200,000 but Small's decision to make it in black and white militated against its success and it was little seen by either audiences or critics. Undeterred, United Artists publicists challenged the public with an advertisement that asked, 'Do you have the courage to spend 83 minutes in *The Tower of London*?' Rather more than courage would have been needed, since the film ran for only 79 minutes.

Story

The evil Richard of Gloucester murders his way to the throne of England.

Price and Corman do their best with the weak script, art director Dan Haller reprises his tried and true Poetic cobwebbed castle corridors, but the film's impact is muted.

'Corny historical melodrama, involving unconvincing ghosts and, apart from a scene or two in the torture dungeon, introducing little that is horrific. Trite and unconvincing, and sadly lacking in excitement, it is likely to disappoint all except easily pleased fans, though title and star appeal provide some draw.'
CEA Film Report

'More bunk than history, perhaps, but still very entertaining... The opening scenes, graced by unusually literate dialogue, are particularly striking; but thereafter convention begins to take over as the horrid visions multiply. Even so... there is little time to be bored.'
Monthly Film Bulletin

'Collector's item: a genuine Roger Corman cut-price version of *Richard III*. Circa 1962. Possibly the last black and white film by this director. Seeking friendly audience... Despite the script's diverse influences, the dialogue is far above the average quality for low budget pictures... All in all – it is great fun!'
Films and Filming

CREDITS

Tower of London (US 1962)
pc Admiral. A Corman Brothers Production
p Gene Corman **d** Roger Corman
dial d Francis Ford Coppola
w Leo V Gordon, F Amos Powell, James B Gordon
ph Arch R Dalziell **bw**
ed Ronald Sinclair **m** Michael Anderson
79 mins.
Cast: Vincent Price (Richard of Gloucester), Michael Pate (Sir Ratcliffe), Joan Freeman (Lady Margaret), Robert Brown (Sir Justin), Justice Watson (Edward IV), Sara Selby (Queen Elizabeth), Richard McCauly (Clarence), Eugene Martin (Prince Edward), Donald Losby (Prince Richard), Sandra Knight (Mistress Shore), Richard Hale (Tyrus), Bruce Gordon (Earl of Buckingham), Joan Camden (Anne)

THE YOUNG RACERS

I had the greatest staff I ever had on The Young Racers.
Roger Corman

The defiantly workaholic Corman decided to take a working vacation as he had done six years previously when he had made *Naked Paradise* and *She Gods of Shark Reef* while allegedly holidaying in Hawaii with his cast and crew.

Backstory

'AIP were going to make a picture during June', Corman said. 'It was in the early days of AIP. They had to cancel at the last minute because they didn't have enough money to make the picture. And I had committed this time and working all the time and I said, "Fellas, I have cleared this time and now you are saying you don't have the money." And I said, "How much do you have?" and they said, "All we have is about $90,000." And I said, "What if I can make something for $90,000?" and they said, "Fine!"

So Bob Campbell, who is a good friend of mine and who had written *Prehistoric World*, had what I thought was a good script about a bullfighter. And I said, "Bob, could you change that script about a bullfighter and make him a Grand Prix racer?" because I was interested in Grand Prix racing. He thought about it, and said "Yeah".

So I said to AIP "I can go to Europe and give you a Grand Prix Formula 1 racing picture for $90,000", and they said "there's no way you can do it". I said, "Look, I have already talked to a couple of guys, and I know the races go on *every other* week." So I told everybody, "We

are not just going to Europe to make a picture. This is an all-expenses-paid vacation. We are going to work *every other* week." We opened at Monte Carlo at the Grand Prix and spent a week there. Then everybody had a week's vacation and met a week later in Rouen in France for the French Grand Prix, we shot all that week and we took the next week off, and went to Spa in Belgium for the Belgian Grand Prix, and so the film was essentially a vacation in Europe.'

R Wright Campbell, brother of actor William Campbell, played his brother's brother and told *Filmfax*, 'I was awful. I was an awful actor. At the time that I did *The Young Racers* I had an excuse for it because I had developed Bell's Palsy so that part of my face was paralysed and it was very difficult to act with half your face.' *The Young Racers* also served as first-rate training in the field for several future graduates of the Roger Corman Academy of Filmmaking.

'Back in the early 1960s, I bought some Russian science fiction movies for practically nothing, and I wanted someone to work on them as a film editor', Corman recalled in 1975. 'I called the U.C.L.A. cinema school and asked them to send over their brightest students. About five kids showed up and I picked Francis (Coppola). He was with me for about a year, doing odd jobs around the office, and I was particularly impressed with him when I let him direct new footage for one of the Russian pictures, called *Battle Beyond the Sun* and he

The Young Racers – a film that was 'essentially a vacation in Europe'

devised two very original monsters, one shaped like a penis and the other like a vagina. So I took Francis to Europe with me to work on *The Young Racers* as my sound man and production assistant. Francis was very good with electronics, however, and he knew something about it: he was not trained but he knew a reasonable amount', Corman said, and commented, 'I had the greatest staff I ever had on *The Young Racers*. Francis Coppola was my Number One assistant, Menachem Golan was Number Two and Bob Towne was Number Three, and the star of the picture was Mark Damon who has gone on to be a producer and distributor.'

Coppola was clearly a fast student and made his directorial debut with *Dementia 13 / The Haunted and the Hunted* which he filmed in Ireland with key cast members from *The Young Racers*, William Campbell, Luana Anders and Patrick Magee. 'I was just the producer', Corman told me. 'Francis wrote and directed it totally. It's totally *his* work. The basis of the idea was mine as to what it was going to be; he simply took my idea for a story and wrote the story and wrote the treatment and then he wrote and directed the script.'

Story

A writer befriends the womanizing Grand Prix racer who seduced his wife with the intention of exposing him in a novel, but comes to realise his intended victim is more sinned against than sinning.

Corman uses his locations to good effect, the racing sequences are exciting, the story, dialogue and acting are rather less so in one of his last obviously B feature movies.

Reviews

'Trite auto racing meller. B.O. range limited. People don't talk or behave in the way they do in *The Young Racers*. Not even young racers, for that matter. So, on the fair assumption that people come to see people when they go to see a film, the Roger Corman production is a limited boxoffice entry in spite of its youthful cast and exploitable topic, which ordinarily might have some solid value for ozone or saturation bookings. The American International release simply doesn't have what it takes. The picture's serious ailments can be traced directly to R Wright Campbell's contrived, affected, pretentious scenario. The dialogue is incredibly stilted

and artificial, and there is too much of it... There are some very pretty girls in this film, which helps immeasurably. In addition to Miss Anders, there are Marie Versini, Beatrice Altariba, Margreta Robsahn and Christina Gregg. Producer-director Corman certainly has an eye for beauty. Too bad he doesn't in this instance have as good an eye for script.'
Variety

'The story, a blend of vanity, rivalry in love and reunion, is not very interesting, but the film scores on its many car-racing sequences in which the perils of top-speed events are authentically set in several famous European racetrack locales, including Aintree. These provide plenty of action and excitement, and the overall result is acceptable supporting entertainment – especially since motor-racing stories are infrequent today so that the subject is unhackneyed.'
CEA Film Report

'In spite of an indifferent cast (William Campbell excepted), good location shooting around the Grand Prix races all over Europe and lively direction by Roger Corman manage to lend a surprising amount of conviction to this weakly plotted tale. For the rest, there is a great deal of pretentious dialogue, and a monumentally silly sequence at and near Aintree, with tea on the lawn, some sort of high society manners, and Patrick Magee and Christina Gregg as a couple of characters straight out of some bastard offspring of *Kind Hearts and Coronets*.'
Monthly Film Bulletin

'This is a very slight film, made, one guesses, mainly for teenagers, despite its 'twist', the characterization is pretty primary... I don't think though that this film reflects Corman's real potentialities... Indeed, one sometimes wishes he could get his scenarios to move as fast as his production teams must do. *The Young Racers* is either too slow for what it has to say, or too thin for its pace... By adroit and occasionally elegant use of locations and their colours Corman and Crosby create a sense of high life truer than in most A-features... As often in Corman's non-horror films, the acting has a nonchalance which is often fresh, often wooden... On the whole this tedious film has too many hints of quality for us to lose faith in the director. But he must, now, get away from Z budgets.'
Films and Filming (May 1964)

'...manages to catch a viewer's attention and hold it to the end. It does this by basic cinematic methods – a way of placing the camera at a natural but effective angle, a technique of shifting the view from one shot to another in a fluid but interesting way. This directorial skill, which may be defined as a simple instinct for moviemaking, extends into the realm of dramatic continuity. Somehow as the film progresses, its superficial protagonists grow more complex and assume added dimensions, until they unexpectedly emerge as interesting people... it is enough to make a viewer wonder what Mr Corman might accomplish with a better project and adequate means.'
The New York Post

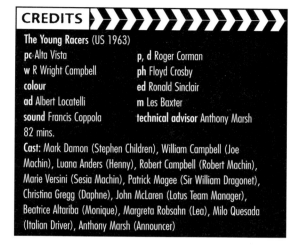

CREDITS

The Young Racers (US 1963)
pc Alta Vista
w R Wright Campbell
colour
ad Albert Locatelli
sound Francis Coppola
82 mins.
p, d Roger Corman
ph Floyd Crosby
ed Ronald Sinclair
m Les Baxter
technical advisor Anthony Marsh

Cast: Mark Damon (Stephen Children), William Campbell (Joe Machin), Luana Anders (Henny), Robert Campbell (Robert Machin), Marie Versini (Sesia Machin), Patrick Magee (Sir William Dragonet), Christina Gregg (Daphne), John McLaren (Lotus Team Manager), Beatrice Altariba (Monique), Margreta Robsahn (Lea), Milo Quesada (Italian Driver), Anthony Marsh (Announcer)

'Prospective high grossing horror comedy melodrama.'

Corman returned to Poe for the fifth time with *The Raven*. *Tales of Terror* had been highly successful and had taken some $1.5 million at the box-office. By now Corman was tired of taking a Gothic approach to Poe and, encouraged by the popularity of *The Black Cat* episode, decided instead to employ a similar blend of comedy and horror in *The Raven*.

As it turned out, the emphasis was firmly on the former.

That was a fun picture because everybody laughed and joked. I think The Raven *was my favourite picture and the most fun*

because I was able to work with three such talented giants of horror films.
Hazel Court

Backstory

'I have always felt *The Raven*, for a three-week shoot, is one of the most accomplished films I directed. Danny Haller again created lavish-looking, stylised sets that gave the film great-looking production values', said Corman.

Ideal casting reunited Price and Lorre and co-starred them with Boris Karloff (who had appeared with Price

The Raven

in *Tower of London* in 1939) and who was now making his first film for AIP. Price was a past master at playing comedy.

Said Corman: 'Vincent was surprisingly adept at humour. His abilities along these lines were put to the test in *The Raven*, a film intended to combine horror with comedy. Vincent's contribution of jokes and comic bits to the shooting script added greatly to the picture's overall humorous effect.'

Lorre, too, was at home with humour. 'I enjoyed working with Lorre. He was one of the best improvisational actors I've ever worked with. He would start with the script and bring so many original ideas and concepts of his own to it that he made every scene that he played better than the script.' But Lorre's habit of ad-libbing did not sit well with Karloff who became increasingly unhappy since he expected the scenes to be played as written. Fortunately, Price was able to satisfy Karloff's need for certainty in their scenes together and also to adapt to Lorre's unexpected additions to the script.

Richard Matheson told *Fangoria*: 'In writing *The Raven*, I didn't even have an original story to work with. They gave me a *poem*. I really had to start from scratch there.' So, according to Price, did the actors. 'The original script of *The Raven* was supposed to have comedy overtones; that is, it was a lot straighter than it finally finished up. And Boris, Peter and I got together and read it through and decided that it didn't make any sense at all. So then we all sort of dreamed up the broader laughs.' Price came up with the effective slapstick idea of hitting his head with the telescope in his study to ensure the audience realised that this time Poe was being played strictly for laughs. Corman's reported greater concern for establishing his set-ups and camera movement than for the needs of actors was commented upon by Karloff, who was quoted in *Films and Filming* as saying: 'Vincent Price, Peter Lorre and I had to find our own way, because Corman had all he wanted. He said, "You're experienced actors, get on with it. I've got the lighting and my angles. I know how I'm going to put this together.' And if you asked him about advice on a scene he'd say, 'That's your pigeon. Go on. I'm busy with this."'

Hammer favourite Hazel Court appeared in the film and juvenile lead Jack Nicholson, whom Corman knew from acting classes and from his over-the-top cameo in *The Little Shop of Horrors*. Said Nicholson: 'Roger gave me one direction on that picture: "Try and be as funny

as Lorre, Karloff and Price".' (He wasn't). He also recalled that the eponymous bird continually fouled the studio. 'It just shit endlessly', said Nicholson. 'My whole right shoulder was constantly covered with raven shit.'

Corman was pleased with Nicholson's contribution: 'I always liked what he did in *The Raven* and he was very good with Peter [Lorre].'

The Raven became Corman's most successful Poe picture so far.

Story

Two rival sixteenth-century English sorcerers engage in a duel of magic while a third is transformed into a raven.

Poe provides the title but not much less for a very funny genre spoof with a witty screenplay ('Where else?' responds Lorre when Price informs him that he keeps his late wife in a coffin in the living room) and relaxed to-the-point direction that showcases the leads who clearly enjoy themselves playing against type. The climactic battle is engaging and collectors of atypical early performances can relish Nicholson's blithely wooden acting. Proof that combining horror and comedy is not as simple as it may seem is provided by the subsequent teaming of Price, Lorre and Karloff in *The Comedy of Terrors* which never manages to reach the sublime heights of *The Raven*.

Reviews

'Prospective high grossing horror comedy melodrama. Poe might turn over in his crypt at this nonsensical adaptation of his immortal poem, but audiences will find the spooky goings-on of a flock of fifteenth-century English sorcerers as envisioned in this Roger Corman production... a cornpop of considerable comedic dimensions... the Richard Matheson screenplay is a skilful, imaginative narrative of what comes to pass when there comes a rapping at magician Vincent Price's chamber door by a raven... Corman as producer-director takes this premise and develops it expertly as a horror-comedy... special effects figure prominently to add sometimes spectacular interest when the two hurl their talents at each other and Les Baxter's musical score is another assist in adding an eerie touch... technical credits generally are superlative.'
Variety

'Though not without its touches of the horrific, this blend of the gay and the gruesome is a largely light-hearted skit on the macabre, with occult trickery and parlour magic mainly played for laughs and reaching its height in the final duel of magic in which the 'weapons' are coloured light rays flashing from the fighters' fingers! On the thrill side are corpses in trucks, sliding door panels and similar time-honoured bogey-bogey para-phernalia. In general, the whole thing is rather a lark fashioned for popular audiences and, with a cast headed by three star exponents of the horror film, is a very use-ful offering of its kind as part of a double programme.'
CEA Film Report

'Although the Gothic castle settings and decorations look very reminiscent of all Corman's earlier Poe films, *The Raven* starts off with the inestimable advantage of a script which not only makes it amply clear from the outset that he is cheerfully and wholeheartedly sending himself up, but manages to do it wittily... the final duel... both wittily and imaginatively staged.' *Monthly Film Bulletin*

'Strictly a picture for the kiddies and the bird-brained; quote the critic.'
The New York Times

'A sappy little parody of a horror picture cutely calculat-ed to make the children scream with terror while their parents scream with glee.'
Time

'More comedy than horror, having little or nothing to do with Poe.'
Castle of Frankenstein

'Of all the horror pictures, *The Raven* flaps the wildest wings.'
Newsweek

'Price, Lorre and Karloff perform singly and in tandem like what they are, three seasoned pros who can take a gentle burlesque and play it to the end of its value with-out stretching it past the entertainment point. They are performances, in their own way, that are virtuoso.'
The Hollywood Reporter

CREDITS

The Raven (US 1963)
pc Alta Vista
exec p James H Nicholson, Samuel Z Arkoff
p, d Roger Corman
w Richard Matheson
With thanks to the poem by Edgar Allan Poe
ph Floyd Crosby
colour. Panavison
ed Ronald Sinclair
ad Daniel Haller
cost Marjorie Corso
sfx Pat Dinga
m Les Baxter
mu Ted Coodley
86 mins.
Vincent Price (Dr Erasmus Craven), Peter Lorre (Dr Bedlo), Boris Karloff (Dr Scarabus), Hazel Court (Lenore Craven), Olice Sturgess (Estelle Craven), Jack Nicholson (Rexford Bedlo), Connie Wallace (Maidservant), William Baskin (Grimes), Aaron Saxon (Gort)

'**The Terror** *is a film such as only Roger Corman could have made — or might have wanted to.'*

Corman made *The Little Shop of Horrors* to take advantage of a standing set. Similarly, rather than allow the lavish sets built for *The Raven* to be torn down without further exploitation, he came up with *The Terror*. It is entirely possible that more people have written about this Corman film than have actually seen it.

It was the only completely scripted story in the history of Hollywood film in which there actually is no story... Perhaps that's why they called it The Terror.
Jack Nicholson

Backstory

'There is no story. We had an idea but we changed it after shooting the first section', Corman told me. 'What happened with *The Terror* was I was just finishing *The Raven* and I was supposed to play tennis on a Sunday and it rained. So I was just sitting around the house and I thought of re-using the sets from *The Raven*. So I called Leo Gordon who is who is an actor and writer and a friend of mine, and said, "Come on over. Let's see if we can come up with an idea to re-use the sets on *The Raven*." And we worked out a general storyline. I knew we were only going to have those sets for two days and I had to shoot right away. I said to Leo, "Just write the scenes that are going to be inside the castle. I'll shoot these in two days. Later on we'll write the rest of the script and shoot the rest of the picture." So I went to Vincent Price on the Monday and said, "Vincent, this is what I am going to do — would you like to just work these two days and play the Baron von

Leppe." And he said he would. But he was going on an art tour — he lectured on art — so I went to the next dressing room, went in and talked to Boris. And Boris said yes, so Boris Karloff played the two days.

I was a member of the Directors Guild and my company was signed with the IA, so I shot those two days. I shot, I don't know, 40 pages in two days, I mean we were just going like crazy, everything, all the interiors were shot in those two days. That was all the money I had and that's all the time I had with those sets because the studio was going to re-use the sets and re-use the stage. I had made a deal with Jack Nicholson that he would emerge as the star of the picture but he would work the two days, and his wife, Sandra Knight, would also do the same. Having done this, I had the two days work, Leo wrote the rest of the picture and I figured the only thing to do was to shoot non-union — which I could not do — for the rest of the picture. So I had my ace assistant, Francis Coppola, shoot a couple of days up at Big Sur with Jack and Sandra and Dick Miller. Then he got a deal at Warner Bros. Monte Hellman came in a little bit later when I had a bit more money and shot some more down at Palos Verdes. And then a little later Jack Hill came in and finally, on the final day of shooting, I didn't have a director and Jack Nicholson said: "Roger, every idiot in town has directed part of this picture. Let me direct the last day." And I said, "Jack, why not?"

We cut the whole thing together and it *was* confusing because the story was being revised by each director and a month would go by or two months between shooting

The Terror
1963 A young Napoleonic officer, Jack Nicholson terrorises a witch woman (Dorothy Neumann)

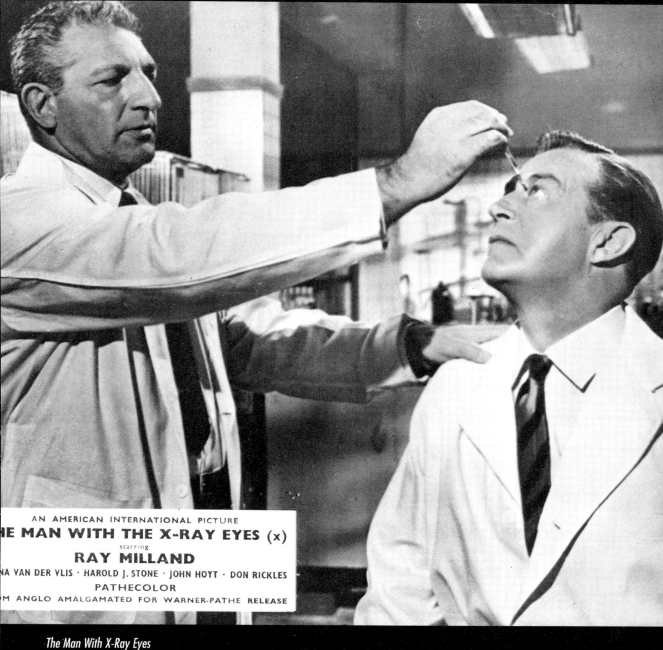

AN AMERICAN INTERNATIONAL PICTURE
HE MAN WITH THE X-RAY EYES (x)
starring
RAY MILLAND
NA VAN DER VLIS · HAROLD J. STONE · JOHN HOYT · DON RICKLES
PATHECOLOR
M ANGLO AMALGAMATED FOR WARNER-PATHE RELEASE

The Man With X-Ray Eyes
1963 Ray Milland gets the special vision treatment from Harold J Stone

GENERAL FILMS présente : stelt voor : American International

RAY MILLAN

MISTER RAYO

"THE MAN WITH THE X-RAY EYES"

X-STRAAL

EDICOLOR — Bruxelles — Tél. : 54.78.71

s X

DIANA van der VLIS · HAROLD J. STONE · JOHN HOYT and DON RICKLES
Prod. & Dir. by ROGER CORMAN · Ex. Prod. JAMES H. NICHOLSON and SAMUEL Z. ARKOFF · Music LES BAXTER

OGEN   TECHNICOLOR®
SPECTARAMA

Imprimé en Belgique

Story

A medical researcher uses himself as a guinea pig in experiments to give himself X-ray vision and is driven insane by its progressive effects.

For all its budgetary and special effects limitations and 'naked' visions that uncomfortably recall contemporary nudie films, Corman's powerful and disturbing science fiction thriller is consistently intriguing, Milland gives one of his finest later performances and the final shot is a terrifying.

Reviews

'Slick programmer with science fiction mixed with chase scenes; treats too many aspects skimpily but has exploitation handles. American International has enough exploitation handles in this sci-fi thriller, with some philosophic aspects and more suggested and justified nudey-comico scenes to have this shaping a good pro-grammer. Film has fine technical assets... there are many interesting comic, dramatic and philosophical ideas are touched on but treated only on the surface. However, director Roger Corman keeps this moving... Special effects on his prism-eye world, called Spectarama, are good if sometimes repetitive. In short, an above average sci-fi thriller with a better technical envelope to pay off commensurably.'
Variety

'This science-fiction tale is unusual and makes a change from run-of-the-mill horror stories. There are many exciting moments, a gory operation and the climax is guaranteed to provide a jolt. Some comedy relief is pro-vided by the doctor as only he can see his fellow dancers at a party twisting in the nude. All the colours of the rainbow add to the camera hokum and ugly psy-chology, but the star carries it with painful skill.'
CEA Film Report

'A horribly gruesome picture which will fascinate the horror fans and turn the stomachs of the squeamish.'
The Hollywood Reporter

'Like the best of macabre films, *The Man With the X-Ray Eyes* has a fair measure of suspense... Milland makes a convincing doctor throughout the film and Corman manages to bring some of the minor characters (such as the showman who cashes in on Xavier's propensity for diagnosing illness) surprisingly alive... But the overall conception of the film is poised uneasily between sci-ence fiction and horror, and only the occasional humor-ous touches and gory details are likely to appeal to Corman followers and/or horror addicts.'
Films and Filming

'Surprisingly level-headed and persuasive in its restraint and succinct dialogue... alertly directed and produced, in colour, by Roger Corman, it shapes up as a modern parable. The concept is original and the tone is thought-ful: Mr Milland's speech in a church is both moving and a wrenching eye-opener.'
The New York Times

CREDITS ▶▶▶▶▶▶▶▶▶▶▶▶▶▶▶

X – The Man With X-Ray Eyes (US 1963)
(GB: **The Man With the X-Ray Eyes**)

pc Alta Vista.	**exec p** James H Nicholson, Samuel Z Arkoff
p, d Roger Corman	**w** Robert Dillon, Ray Russell
st Ray Russell	**ph** Floyd Crosby
sp ph fx filmed in Spectarama	
ed Anthony Carras	**ad** Daniel Haller
cost Marjorie Corso	**sfx** Butler-Glouner Inc.
m Les Baxter	**mu** Ted Coodley
80 mins.	

Cast: Ray Milland (Dr James Xavier), Diana Van Der Vlis (Dr Diane Fairfax), Harold J Stone (Dr Sam Brant), John Hoyt (Dr Willard Benson), Don Rickles (Crane), John Dierkes (Preacher), Lorrie Summers (Party Dancer), Vicki Lee (Young Girl Patient), Kathryn Hart (Mrs Mart), Dick Miller, Jonathan Haze (Hecklers)

THE HAUNTED PALACE

'Horror, sorcery & return from the dead, with the inevitable Price.'

Corman's next Poe picture *The Haunted Palace* was, in fact, a dramatization of the story *The Strange Case of Charles Dexter Ward* by H P Lovecraft. Only the title owed anything to Poe and it was not, as claimed by AIP, from a story but from one of his poems.

One of the great traps in Hollywood is to buy a very good novel, and then make so many changes that you lose the essence of the novel.
Roger Corman

Backstory

Corman had started planning *The Haunted Palace* (as *The Haunted Village*) while filming *The Premature Burial* and had intended to use Ray Milland, Hazel Court and Boris Karloff. By the time he came to make it, AIP gave Vincent Price and Debra Paget the leading roles and Lon Chaney Jr was cast as a replacement for Karloff who was unwell. 'This was late in the series, when I was saying that I'm beginning to repeat and so forth. I just said I didn't want to do a Poe film and Jim Nicholson and I both liked the work of Lovecraft, who I think is very, very good. For me, Poe is fractionally more interesting, and a more complex writer, but I think Lovecraft is very good in that field and so we decided to do a Lovecraft film,' Corman recalled in 1984. 'I made some gestures towards bringing some Poe into it so that it could be sold, I think, as Poe and Lovecraft, but it was really primarily Lovecraft and it was slightly misleading

advertising...' He also recalled a stylistic innovation. 'I think it was the first film in which I used zoom lenses. They had recently been developed and they were much slower than the normal fixed lens, and as a result you had to pour in the light on the set in order to reach an intensity that a zoom lens could photograph.'

Story

An eighteenth-century New England warlock who is burned at the stake possesses his ancestor 110 years later.

Somewhat stolid but still intriguing, thanks to Corman's psychological approach to the familiar horrors made more familiar by Haller's now somewhat self-referential sets. Still, how can one resist a film which boasts the line, 'Ah yes, Torqemada spent many a happy hour here, a few centuries ago'.

Reviews

'...quite straightforward and easy to follow. The bizarre tale is unfolded in relatively leisurely fashion though with a few shock moments likely to startle, concentrating on macabre atmosphere – effective though relying considerably on dirty weather, with thunderstorms conveniently raging at all climactic moments. Disfigured, zombie-like creatures also play a part in the hokum, which includes other stock horror film ingredients, but well treated and with imaginative sets and colour. Perhaps it is not wildly exciting, but in total effect it

makes polished and reliable entertainment for almost any kind of audience, attracted by macabre entertainment.'
CEA Film Report

'Roger Corman is an old hand at turning out lurid horror melodramas in low-budget colour such as *The Haunted Palace* ... (is) neither better nor worse than such predecessors as *The Pit and the Pendulum*, *The House of Usher*, and *The Premature Burial*. It has the director's usual star (Vincent Price), his usual shock devices (sudden cuts to close-ups emphasising fantastic make-up) and his usual inane dialogue.'
The New York Times

'Horror, sorcery and return from the dead, with the inevitable Price.'
Castle of Frankenstein

'Unpretentious direction, well informed commentary.'
The Cinema

'One of Corman's lesser AIP efforts... A few nice touches of Cormanesque black parody and neat ending. Beautiful opening titles.'
Castle of Frankenstein

'Disappointingly, the decor looks very *déjà vu*: here are those endless stone passages lovingly hung with cobwebs and shadows, ornately gloomy chambers with creaking doors, and exteriors perpetually shrouded in ground fogs, which Daniel Haller has provided for other Corman adaptations from Poe, again shot in those slightly musty colours. *The Haunted Palace* would, in fact, be a rather routine Corman were it not for the narrative drive and invention.'
Monthly Film Bulletin

CREDITS ▷▷▷▷▷▷▷▷▷▷▷▷▷

The Haunted Palace (US 1963)
pc Alta Vista   **p, d** Roger Corman
w Charles Beaumont
From The Strange Case of Charles Dexter Ward by H P Lovecraft and the title of the poem by Edgar Allan Poe
ph Floyd Crosby   **colour.** Panavision
ed Ronald Sinclair   **ad** Daniel Haller
mu Ted Coodley   **m** Ronald Stein
titles Armand Acosta   85 mins.
Cast: Vincent Price (Charles Dexter Ward/Joseph Curwen), Debra Paget (Ann Ward), Lon Chaney Jr (Simon Orne), Frank Maxwell (Dr Marinus Willet), Leo Gordon (Edgar Weeden), Elisha Cook Jr (Peter Smith), John Dierkes (Jacob West), Harry Ellerbe (Minister), Cathy Merchant (Hester Tillinghast), Milton Parsons (Jaber Hutchinson), Guy Wilkerson (Leach), Darlene Lucht (Young Victim), Barboura Morris (Mrs Weeden), Bruno Ve Sota (Bartender)

HESTER
TILLINGHAST

1723 - 1791

THE SECRET INVASION

Corman hadn't fought a celluloid war since his first, *Ski Troop Attack,* in 1960 when he interrupted his series of Poe adaptations and went to Yugoslavia to make *The Secret Invasion.*

I was trying to make a very big-looking film in 36 days on $500,000. It was just too tough.
Roger Corman

Backstory

The Secret Invasion was funded by United Artists and produced by Gene Corman and was Corman's first film for a major studio. The budget of $600,000 was his largest to date – Corman had been making *two* Poe pictures for the same price. It was written (as *The Dubious Patriots* which UA changed to *The Secret Invasion*) by R Wright Campbell who had scripted *The Young Racers* and had a storyline was presciently similar in theme to *The Dirty Dozen* – except that it preceded Robert Aldrich's overblown blockbuster by some four years and, indeed, Campbell had come up with much the same plot for Corman's 1955 Western *Five Guns West.* Filming on a six-week schedule in Yugoslavia turned out to be a fraught affair. Corman not only had to cope with the complex logistical problems and unforseen glitches involved in making a film on location but he also had to deal with the ego of his leading actor

Stewart Granger who decided, on the wing, that he wanted his role inflated with a line originally assigned to co-star Edd Byrne. Corman smoothed out the situation and succeeded in bringing in *The Secret Invasion* on time and, at $592,000, under budget as well.

When, in 1979, I spent two and a half hellish weeks holed up with Stewart Granger in his almost unfurnished Beverly Hills-style hacienda in Spain during an, as it turned out, abortive attempt to ghost his autobiography, I unwisely mentioned Corman in conversation. Granger was still incensed by the fact that Roger and Gene had shared a hotel room to ensure that as much of the budget as possible ended up on the screen, not on overheads.

Corman told me: 'Stewart Granger was the most difficult actor I ever had to work with in my life, yet at the same time his performance was very good, I will say that for him. ...It was the first film I think he had done away from a major. He had been a big star at MGM and he was slipping a little bit and he knew it and it was a come-down for him to do an independent film. And then when he realised how low budget the independent film *was,* much lower than he ever thought, I think there were a lot of psychological things working there.'

In the event, *The Secret Invasion* took some $3 million at the box-office.

Story

A British major recruits five convicted criminals whose special talents he needs to rescue an Italian general held by the Nazis in a fortress in Dubrovnik.

Corman moves the proceedings at a brisk clip that compensates for occasional lacunae in characterisation and dialogue, stages vivid and visceral action and pulls off a fashionably downbeat ending.

Reviews

'In outline, this is just another of those wartime adventures in which reluctant heroes bring off some daring coup to bring victory one step nearer; in detail, however, it is a very different matter, for Corman has cast his highly idiosyncratic spell over the film... the film has an intense formal beauty which runs unnervingly counter to the brutalities of its story... where *The Secret Invasion* scores particularly heavily, in fact, is in its brilliantly imaginative use of detail.'
Monthly Film Bulletin

'This is a fast-moving war adventure which has an abundance of action, plenty of suspense, moments of gory combat and violence, and large-scale battle scenes which are convincingly and spectacularly staged. The story has some unexpected twists and, with only the merest hint of romance and humour, makes no concessions to relief; it is daring exploits and adventure all the way, and as such should well appeal to devotees of war films.'
CEA Film Report

'It operates well enough on a routine level but its failure to be anything more than a passable adventure must disappoint those who set a high store by Corman's work... there is a disturbing casualness about Corman's overall handling. It reminds one that his basic style, evolved in low-budget quickies, has been generally conventional and even old-fashioned, though he has learnt to enliven weak material with gorgeous embellishments of pure style. These he can hardly fit to the present film and he has merely followed the script instead of commenting on it. As his own producer, he didn't need to have too weak a script surely – unless he is a less serious artist than we are being told. This is clear progress in a commercial sense, being the biggest film Corman has yet attempted and made in six weeks against natural locations in an unfamiliar country; so all credit, commercially speaking, to what Corman has again achieved in restricting circumstances.'
Films and Filming (March 1965)

'A rather surprising amount of brisk muscularity and panoramic colour, if not always credibility... Although R Wright Campbell's script is tautly triggered for action most of the way, the plot – the rescue of a general from a Nazi fortress – still seems familiar... For the most part, Mr Corman has them on the go, spraying bullets galore... the grim irony of the fadeout holds a good, firm twist. Most impressive of all, however, is the picturesque sweep of the Dalmatian coast, photographed in attractive colour.'
The New York Times

CREDITS ▶▶▶▶▶▶▶▶▶▶▶▶

The Secret Invasion (US 1964)
pc San Carlos Productions
p, d Roger Corman
ph Arthur E Arling
ed Ronald Sinclair
sfx George Blackmell
95 mins.
exec p Gene Corman
w R Wright Campbell
colour. Panavision
ad John Murray
m Hugo Friedhofer

Cast: Stewart Granger (Major Richard Mace), Raf Vallone (Roberto Rocca), Henry Silva (John Durrell), Mickey Rooney (Terrence Scanlon), Edd Byrnes (Simon Fell), William Campbell (Jean Saval), Mia Massini (Mila), Helmo Kindermann (German Fortress Commandant), Enzo Fiermonte (General Quadri), Peter Coe (Marko), Nan Morris (Stephana), Helmut Schneider (German Captain), Giulio Marchetti (Italian Officer), Nicholas Rend (Fishing Boat Captain), Craig March (Petar), Todd Williams (Partisan Leader), Charles Brent (Monk #1), Richard Johns (Wireless Operator), Kurt Bricker (German Naval Lieutenant), Katrina Rozan (Peasant Woman)

The Corman Company
presents

STEWART   RAF   MICKEY   EDD
GRANGER **VALLONE** **ROONEY** **BYRNES**
and HENRY **SILVA** as Durrell
in
"**THE SECRET INVASION**" (A)
introducing MIA MASSINI

Produced by Gene Corman
Directed by Roger Corman
Colour by De Luxe
Panavision

UNITED
ARTISTS

Stewart Granger leads *The Secret Invasion*

THE MASQUE OF THE RED DEATH

'Portends good b.o..'

Corman had done some of the pre-production for *The Secret Invasion* in London: he now returned to Britain to make *The Masque of the Red Death* which stands out as the finest of his Poe adaptations and a genre classic.

I thought when it was over that I had possibly gotten a little bit overly philosophical and stepped a little bit away from horror and it should have been more of a horror film.
Roger Corman

Backstory

Corman had wanted to make *The Masque of the Red Death* as his second Poe project after *House of Usher*. James Nicholson, however, had consistently opted for *The Pit and the Pendulum* and, Corman told *Films and Filming*, 'Each picture afterward, they would say, "What do you think?" and each time I would give them two choices, and one of them would be *Masque of the Red Death* and we kept staying away from it and staying away from it until late in the cycle, we finally did it.'
Sam Arkoff had a co-production deal with Anglo-Amalgamated who distributed AIP's films in Britain which gave Corman the opportunity to make *Masque of the Red Death* on a long (for him) five-week schedule although, in comparison to American crews, the highly unionized British technicians were less flexible. Corman told me that the only major difference he found working in a British studio: 'was, I felt, that the English crews were a little bit slower than the American crews, but the quality of work was just as good. I *did* feel that I did not have quite the camaraderie with the crew in England that I did in the United States. It may have been the fact

that I was an American and they were British and there was a slight cultural thing. But I also feel there is a little more stratification in English society than in American society and the crew wasn't quite ready to accept the director as one of them the way an American crew would. I think there was just a little bit of that "them versus us" but basically I got along with them. But I could see I didn't have – I'll use that word again – the camaraderie that I had with an American crew or the feeling that we were all in this together to make a film. Nevertheless, they did very good work and I was pleased with the result.'

Mind you, according to Sam Arkoff, Corman succeeded in outflanking the unions when, realising he was running out of time filming the climactic masque, he shot the rehearsal. The unions were outraged but Corman had the sequence. Pre-eminent among the crew was cinematographer Nicolas Roeg. 'He's an excellent cameraman,' Corman told interviewer Christopher Wicking, 'and created some very good effects. What happens generally is that I pick the angles, positions and movements of the camera, suggest lenses and give the cameraman a lighting "theme", a colour feeling I want for the scene, whether it's dark and sombre or much lighter – and Nic lit everything really very beautifully.'

Roeg's contribution was complemented by Daniel Haller's evocative production design which benefitted considerably from the fact that Haller was able to use existing scenery and props from the Associated British Picture Corporation's Elstree Studios. 'The one thing I *did* get in England, particularly with *Masque of the Red Death*, I got a bigger "look", I got bigger sets,' Corman told me. 'They had a tremendous scene dock. Danny Haller the art director and I went through the scene dock and we saw flats from – I don't remember whether it was *Becket* or *A Man for All Seasons* but pictures like that. The work was just far better and far grander than anything we ever had to work with in the United States, so I go a much bigger look.' Corman wrote the original treatment with Charles Beaumont but when he looked at the resulting screenplay, he was unhappy with the result.

Corman brought in R Wright Campbell, who recalled: 'I then got the idea of taking another Poe story, *Hop Frog*, and putting the two of them together... it was one of his classics.' Campbell had never worked on one of the Poe films but was, conveniently, in London and the screenplay was rewritten in two weeks, with Corman creating the key concepts of good and evil which were missing from the first screenplay and which were so important to the ultimate power of the film, turning Prospero from a standard evil tyrant into more of a thinker and philosopher. 'In fact, I don't even think of Prospero solely as being evil. It's simply he *chose* evil as a course of action because of what he saw in the world around him. He himself, I would hope, is not a "bad man', maybe just a mistaken one".'

Vincent Price, the ideal choice for Prospero, British small-part actress Jane Asher and Patrick Magee headed the cast and were ideally cast. Corman was rather less fortunate with finally having to cast a girl as the dwarf woman who plays a catalytic role in the drama and then dub her with an adult actress, since Veronica Greenlaw is clearly a young girl instead of an adult dwarf. 'What it amounted to was you solve the problem as best you can,' Corman told me. 'It was essential to me that the little dwarf be beautiful or at least extremely attractive, and frankly I couldn't find one in casting. As so the only solution finally seemed to be to get a very good-looking little girl.'

Corman's problems did not end with the completion of the picture. The then unliberal British censor took offence at elements of devil worship in the film. In 1964, Corman told British film critic Alexander Walker, 'The Masque of the Red Death* was one of a series of pictures I'd done on the works of Edgar Allan Poe. These pictures were treated as horror pictures and were subject to a certain amount of censorship previously. *Masque of the Red Death,* however, had probably less horror than

any of the others and was censored to the greatest extent. The reason for that was not horror, as such, but the fact that we did have Satanism in the picture and John Trevelyan who is the British censor, stated that there was a problem in England today to do with Satanism,' and then added when we spoke in 1997, 'There was nothing in *Masque of the Red Death* that I could think in any way you should cut.'

He summed up the film in *Fangoria*: '*Masque* is more philosophical. We were dealing with the plague, and it was fear of death *per se*, not fear of any violence. It was not what AIP wanted though.' It was, however, exactly what filmgoers and most of the more sniffy of the critics who had yet to come to appreciate his work, wanted.

Story
A devil-worshipping prince holes up in his castle in twelfth-century Italy hoping to avoid the plague that is ravaging the country but Death finally catches up with him and his corrupt followers.

Corman's atmospheric, visually ravishing Gothic story is a genre masterpiece. The screenplay is literate and intriguing, the period dialogue strikes few false notes and the storyline does not shy away from telling intellectual concepts of good and evil and Price's serious and sustained performance ranks among his best. Corman's creative imagination and powerful narrative drive never falter, his vivid deployment of detail potentiates the growing ambience of macabre unease and he succeeds in deliberately echoing Bergman and *The Seventh Seal* in his presentation of Death without allowing himself to fall victim to accusations of either plagiarism or sycophancy. His finest film.

Reviews
'Portends good b.o. Latest catches the flavour of past offerings in this field of horror and exploitation and should carry the same lure, particularly with the name of Vincent Price, star of most of AIP's Poe programme, to build on. Roger Corman, responsible for the majority of former entries here, again produces and directs. He has garmented his film, lensed in England, with production values. His colour camera work, his sets, music and plot unfoldment itself – if the latter is vague and a bit involved it still fits into the pattern intended – establish an appropriate mood for the pic's tale of terror and in addition it's evident Corman doesn't take his subject too

seriously... Corman in his direction sets a pace calculat-
ed to divert the teenage taste particularly, and past experience with Poe makes him a worthy delineator of this
master of the macabre. In Price is the perfect inter-
preter, too, of the Poe character, and he succeeds in creating an aura of terror... Art direction, by Robert Jones
and lensing by Nicholas Roeg are particular standouts,
giving class to the pic, and David Lee's music score suitably backdrops the action.'
Variety

'...this many-hued fantasy is in the best traditions of
creepy hokum; it is fairly spine-chilling, has the benefit
of good production and macabre mounting, colourful
settings and costumes and star domination by Vincent
Price. It is let down only by patches of corny dialogue
which might raise laughter in some locations, but otherwise it is effective entertainment for lovers of horrific-
style thrillers.'
CEA Film Report

'A story of evil; of Satanism and devil worship.. A story
that chills the eye even as it fascinates... A story to evoke
loathing and contempt... *The Masque of the Red Death* is
the sixth in the Edgar Allan Poe series directed by
American Roger Corman, and it will probably be
acclaimed as his best. The sets are superb... (and) have
the shocking authenticity of the frightful cult of
Satanism. Colour highlights the all-pervading air of evil.
Vincent Price is a magnificent Prince Prospero, epito-
mizing the unregenerate worshipper of Satan. Hazel
Court gives an eerie portrayal of the female of the same
species.'
ABC Film Review

'It is by far the most ambitious film made by Corman,
as well as being the most interesting in the choice of
subject and the way in which it is handled... The style:
boldly cinematic and full of wonderfully realized effects.
I can't recall when I've seen such a collection of pan-
ning shots; or where I've seen (outside a Minnelli or
Cukor film) such a stylized use of colour before...
Visually the film is stunning (thanks in no small part to
Nicholas Roeg's superb colour photography and Robert
Jones' imaginative art direction), almost, if not quite,
Gothic in its imagery... *The Masque of the Red Death*
strikes me as being a film to cheer for. Not great (with a

capital G) but good (with a capital G).'
Films and Filming (August 1964)

'Corman's major Poe adaptation; stylish, imaginatively written, more symbolic than previous films in the series, and more of a personal statement. Weakness is in uneven structure of seriousness and parody, several unusual filmic experiments which really don't come to fruition. We still like *Tomb of Ligeia* best of all, but *Masque* has enough fine moments to make it a classic in years to come.'
Castle of Frankenstein

'Unquestionably Roger Corman's best film to date, *The Masque of the Red Death* has passages of such real distinction that one wishes he could be persuaded to take himself more seriously. Not, one hastens to add, that he should turn to more 'serious' subjects or stifle the bursts of sardonic humour that go hand in hand with Vincent Price, but rather that he should dispense with the crude shock effects which occasionally (notably in the dungeon scenes) mar a film which elsewhere operates on a much subtler level... *The Masque of the Red Death* is graced with an uncommonly intelligent script which probes the concept of diabolism with considerable subtlety... At times, in fact, the film reminds one of *The Seventh Seal* in its intellectual probings, in its figuration of Death, and, particularly, the conception of the final sequence.'
Monthly Film Bulletin

'... represents the dauntless young filmmaker at the top of his form... it is a cheap and stylish horror melodrama, very freely based on an Edgar Allan Poe tale according to the genre Mr Corman has been specializing in for years... the film is vulgar, naive and highly amusing, and it is played with gusto by Mr Price, Hazel Court and Jane Asher. As for Mr Corman, he has let his imagination run riot upon a mobile decor scheme. The result may be loud, but it looks like a real movie. On its level, it is astonishingly good.'
The New York Times

'Corman may yet out-horror all the horror filmmakers.'
The New York Daily News

CREDITS ▶▶▶▶▶▶▶▶▶▶▶▶▶

The Masque of the Red Death (GB 1964)
pc Alta Vista/Anglo Amalgamated   **p, d** Roger Corman
assoc p George Willoughby
w Charles Beaumont, R Wright Campbell
From the stories Masque of the Red Death and Hop Toad by Edgar Allen Poe

ph Nicolas Roeg	**Colour.** Panavision
ed Ann Chegwidden	**p** design Daniel Haller
ad Robert Jones	**cost** Laura Nightingale
sfx George Blackwell	**m** David Lee
choreo Jack Carter	**mu** George Partleton
86 mins.	

Cast: Vincent Price (Prince Prospero), Hazel Court (Juliana), Jane Asher (Francesca), David Weston (Gino), Patrick Magee (Alfredo), Nigel Green (Ludovico), Skip Martin (Hop Toad), John Westbrook (Man in Red), Julian Burton (Senor Veronese), Doreen Dawn (Anna-Marie), Paul Whitsun-Jones (Scarlatti), Jean Lodge (Scarlatti's Wife), Verina Greenlaw (Esmeralda), Brian Hewlett (Lampredi), Harvey Hall (Clistor), Robert Brown (Guard)

THE TOMB OF LIGEIA

> '...the most sensitive of the Poe stories that Corman has directed.'

Corman and Price remained in England to make their final film together, *The Tomb of Ligeia*. It was also the last of Corman's Poe adaptations, and while the series ended on a high note the film, almost inevitably, did not quite reach the heights achieved by *Masque of the Red Death*.

They asked me to do one after the other and finally I stopped. They wanted me to continue but I just said that I had done enough of them.
Roger Corman

Backstory

As written by Robert Towne, who had served as both screenwriter and actor *The Last Woman on Earth* and had been involved in *The Young Racers* and would go on to win an Academy Award for *Chinatown*, *The Tomb of Ligeia* was more Gothic romance than straightforward horror movie. When AIP cast Vincent Price as the tortured protagonist rather than a conventional leading man the perception of the film, if not its balance, was inevitably tipped towards the latter. Towne later expressed his unhappiness with this choice, having had conceived the role in terms of a younger actor. ('The original concept was for a very dashing, romantic, handsome, young leading man, which Vincent played in his youth and could have played'). '*Ligeia* was a *very* short story,' said Towne, ' and I felt the best thing to do would be to take Poe's themes and expand on them.' His final screenplay included elements of mesmerism and necrophilia which he found in Poe. *The Tomb of Ligeia*

was unique in that, for the first time in his Poe cycle, Corman made the film on location, noting: 'For the first time the sun shone on the works of Edgar Allan Poe.'

The complex nature of the central theme of possession made filming difficult. Said Corman: 'It became extremely complex at the end. As a matter of fact, I remember I had written into the back of my script a little chart of the changes and I hate to say I don't remember exactly, but there was a concept where – was her name Rowena? – would lose possession of her body and the Lady Ligeia would return to take possession, then Rowena would regain possession of her body. So it was a tale of Ligeia coming from the grave to reclaim her previous life and her husband through the current wife. And what became very complex was the rapidity and method in which Ligeia would return to take over the body of Rowena. I remember I actually had to have a chart that I wrote one night as I was in the middle of one scene. I said, "Exactly where are we?" And I had to stop for a minute and look back at the script to rechart what was going on.'

The birth pangs may have been painful but the result was subtle, strange and dreamlike and very much in line with the Freudian views he expressed in an interview with screenwriter Christopher Wicking and Vincent Porter: 'I find myself working more and more on the concept of the unconscious. And I find that I put things into my pictures that I'm not aware of. I looked recently at some films I made a few years ago and I saw things I didn't realise were there when I actually made them. It

seems to be then that you worked to a certain degree
on a conscious level. I've studied a fair amount of Freud
so I think I know to an extent what my symbols mean,
but for me the beauty of it all is that there is a symbolism at work *behind* your own symbolism so what you
thought you mean in fact means something else.'

The pressbook for the film confirmed his approach.
'You don't have to be an egghead to enjoy the new Poe
terror film', it proclaimed, 'but an understanding of psy-
chology helps,' according to its director Roger Corman.
While most movie fans are familiar with the menacing
roles played by Vincent Price, Corman declares that
'enjoyment of the Poe films in which Price has been
starring recently is greatly enhanced if you are acquaint-
ed with the philosophy of Sigmund Freud.' *The Tomb of
Ligeia* 'actually did make money', Corman told *Fangoria*,
'but it didn't make as much as the previous ones.' When
AIP insisted on returning to Poe without him, the law
of diminishing returns became even more evident and
confirmed Corman's view that 'I was just wearing out
on this series.'

Story

**A drug-addicted nineteenth-century widower
marries again but is morbidly convinced that his
dead wife is still alive.**

Corman's exemplary use of locations, eerily photographed by Hammer Films regular Arthur Grant, adds
intensity to the bizarre brew of necrophilia, mesmerism
and obsessive romance. Price is suitably serious and
haunted, and Corman's stylish handling and ingenious
use of Freudian symbolism illuminates Poe's frequent
theme of life after death and makes it one of the more
atmospheric and chilling films in the Poe series,
although Corman is not always able to disguise the narrative confusions in Towne's screenplay.

Reviews

'Disappointing pic from Edgar Allan Poe tale; light biz
possible with heavy exploitation push. More Poe but no
go about sums up *The Tomb of Ligeia,* a tedious and talky
addition to American International's series of chill-pix
based on tales by the nineteenth-century US author.
Roger Corman produced and directed a script that
resists analysis and lacks credibility, with all perfor-

imizing gore angles, but it doesn't gel, so neither suspense addicts nor bloodhounds will dig it. Strictly lower-case material but saturation-exploitation bookings might help... Price disappoints in attempt to project character's inner struggle to escape spell since no one knows why he acts kooky... camera work is routine, except for a few setups using abbey walls to frame scenes. Verdant exteriors are pleasant but are so intercut as to destroy what little suspense has been built up on the inside. Music is too busy and totally ineffective, telegraphing every flop shock situation... sole plus factor is opening title work by Francis Rodker who provides artistic and eerie suggestions of quality that doesn't follow.'
Variety

'This latest Corman horror film takes in a fair amount of the English countryside as well as the eerie abbey, and is both picturesque and colourful. There are plenty of horrifying moments, atmosphere is fairly eerie throughout, and the fire climax is a spectacular highlight. Following a similar pattern of horror stories it is well played by the cast, Vincent Price having a serious role this time – the whole thing is played "straight" and without concession to humour. The picture will no doubt be enjoyed by fans of macabre entertainment.'
CEA Film Report

'May not be the best of his (Corman's) series of Edgar Allan Poe divertimenti but it is his most far-out, and, in the last half hour or so, his most concentrated piece of black magic.'
Newsweek

'Though Corman's admirers are unlikely to be too disappointed by his new film, one may still regret the loss of narrative clarity which featured so strongly in *The Masque of the Red Death*. The crowded metamorphoses of the last ten minutes make for a confused climax. Moreover the blinding of Fell, the destruction of the abbey by fire, the blood-stained embrace of the doomed man and his ghostly beloved, are all too reminiscent of earlier Corman films – too much, in fact, of a formulary, melodramatic hotchpotch. Luckily there are ample compensations. The earlier intimations of horror are put over casually and briskly, notable where the black cat is concerned. Much of the incident is genuinely strange...

Technically the film is less accomplished than *The Masque of the Red Death*, but it is still better – certainly more serious and naturalistic – than Corman's Hollywood Poe cycle.'
Monthly Film Bulletin

...and in some ways is probably his best work. Devoid of the gadgetry of *Pit and the Pendulum* or to a lesser extent *Masque of the Red Death*, Corman concentrates on a more subjective treatment of a man's struggle which superficially is against the supernatural but basically is against the fears of being dominated by a stronger willed person, of being forced down, controlled, and eventually submerged. Very impressive.'
Films and Filming March 1965

'Here at last Mr Corman has done what it always seemed he might be able some time to do: make a film which could without absurdity be spoken of in the same breath as Cocteau's *Orphee*.'
The Times

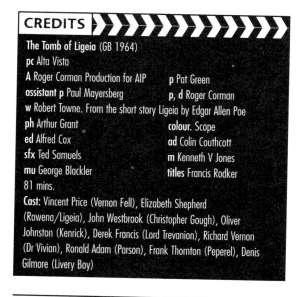

CREDITS

The Tomb of Ligeia (GB 1964)

pc Alta Vista

A Roger Corman Production for AIP

assistant p Paul Mayersberg

w Robert Towne. From the short story Ligeia by Edgar Allen Poe

ph Arthur Grant

ed Alfred Cox

sfx Ted Samuels

mu George Blackler

81 mins.

p Pat Green

p, d Roger Corman

colour. Scope

ad Colin Couthcott

m Kenneth V Jones

titles Francis Rodker

Cast: Vincent Price (Vernon Fell), Elizabeth Shepherd (Rowena/Ligeia), John Westbrook (Christopher Gough), Oliver Johnston (Kenrick), Derek Francis (Lord Trevanion), Richard Vernon (Dr Vivian), Ronald Adam (Parson), Frank Thornton (Peperel), Denis Gilmore (Livery Boy)

The Tomb of Ligeia brought Corman's seminal series of Poe adaptations to a finish and was, until *Frankenstein Unbound* in 1990, his last foray into horror. The subsequent seven films which he directed in the Sixties reflected his sharp talent for grasping and exploiting new cinema trends before they became played out.

Part 4

ANGELS AND VILLAINS

I made two distinct types of movies in the Sixties. First, there were what I call 'studio-like' films, and they would include the Poe adaptations. Then there were the pictures of the times like Wild Angels *and* The Trip.
Roger Corman

Corman succumbed briefly and sadly unproductively to the lure of working with a major studio when, after completing *The Tomb of Ligeia*, he signed with Columbia Pictures in the belief that he would be given the opportunity to make bigger pictures. But his legendary reputation as a maker of highly profitable low-budget movies worked against him and he was simply offered the kind of small-scale projects that he had joined Columbia in order to avoid. After a year, he and Columbia parted company and he returned to AIP – on the understanding that he would not consider a further foray into Poe. Corman felt that he had taken Gothic horror as far as he wanted with his Poe series and, making the accurate assessment that the genre was starting to be played out, once again displayed his enviable ability to stay ahead of the game and his even more enviable talent for breaking new ground by switching to new genres with *The Wild Angels*, the first and one of the best of the spate of Sixties and Seventies exploitation biker movies, which also turned out to be one of AIP's most profitable films.

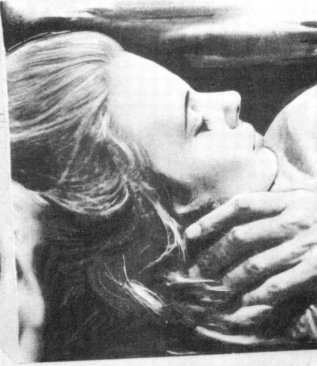

DEZE WEEK:

Les films **KINDEREN NIET TOEGELATEN**
EDDIE DE JONG
S.P.R.L.

Ciné

La Tom
Het Gra

VINCENT PRICE
ELIZABETH SHEPHERD

REGIE: ROGER CORMAN

COLORSCOPE

Prod.:
AMERICAN INTERNATIONAL

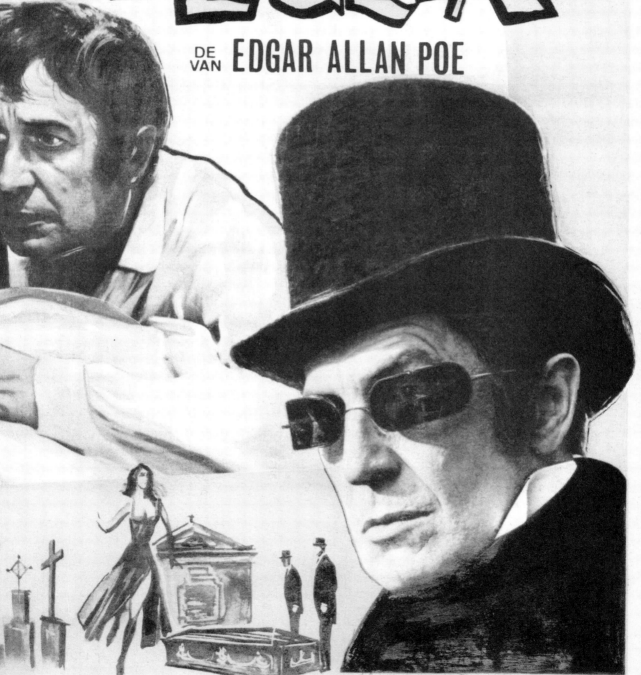

QUELLIN

Uren der vertoningen
2 - 4 - 6 - 8 - 10

BE de
van LIGEIA

DE van EDGAR ALLAN POE

'Realistic leather jacket delinquency yarn.'

The picture you are about to see will shock and perhaps anger you. Although the events and characters are fictitious, the story is a reflection of out times.
The Wild Angels – on-screen disclaimer

Backstory

Corman's inspiration for *The Wild Angels* came from the photograph of a gang of Hell's Angels riding their choppers to the funeral of one of their members, 'Mother' Miles, in the January, 1966 issue of *Life* magazine. The action in the legendary, if overrated, 1954 biker movie *The Wild Ones* (starring Marlon Brando and Lee Marvin as possibly the oldest Hell's Angels in celluloid history) had been told from the point of view of the townspeople who were subjected to the bikers' depredations.

Ever the innovator Corman, who saw Hell's Angels as contemporary cowboys with motorcycles replacing their horses, decided to stage *The Wild Angels* from the point of view of the Hell's Angels and initially reaped the critical whirlwind for his pains.

Frequent collaborator Charles B Griffith was hired to turn Corman's treatment of *All the Fallen Angels* (Jack Nicholson came up with the more commercial title *The Wild Angels*) into a screenplay and the two began their research by going, dressed in appropriately un-Hollywood style, to biker hangouts like *The Gunk Shop* in East Los Angeles. Corman assured the Angels that he was not out to exploit them but intended, instead, to tell their story and gained their confidence, drank, smoked marijuana and socialized with them.

In the event Griffith's screenplay was extensively rewritten and toughened up by Corman protégé Peter Bogdanovich (who also served as Corman's assistant and appeared in a minor role) and his then wife Polly Platt, although Bogdanovich was unable to receive an on-screen credit for his work.

For Bogdanovich, who also worked as Corman's assistant and appeared briefly in a minor role: '*The Wild Angels* was three weeks of the greatest film school anybody could ever put me through. You were doing it, you were under pressure, you had to deliver.'

George Chakiris was slated to play the leading role but when it turned out he was unable to ride a motorcycle and wanted a stunt double, he was out. Corman replaced him with Peter Fonda whom he moved up from a supporting role in which he would have spend most of the time playing a corpse: the part went to Bruce Dern. Fonda accepted after his character's name was changed from Jack Black to Heavenly Blues, which he claimed was slang for morning glory seeds that could be powdered and used as an hallucinogenic. His fee was $10,000.

Corman filmed *The Wild Angels* on a three-week schedule that took the unit to locations in Venice, San Pedro, Mecca, California and the mountains and desert around Palm Springs, paying the real-life Angels from the Venice Chapter $35 a day and an additional $25 for their bikes, and a mere $15 a day for their 'old ladies'.

The problems of the difficult, pressured shoot were compounded by Corman having to deal with the nonprofessional and often feckless Angels.

'I spent some time thinking about how I would direct the Hell's Angels and I finally decided to do it as objectively as possible. I thought, there is no way I am really going to be able to order them to do things, but on the other hand, if I am too weak and *ask* them to do things, they will take advantage of me. So I thought, I will be as impersonal as possible and simply state what has to be done. "Fellas, the bikes come in at that point in the road and you come down here to this point; you are travelling about this fast and you turn and dismount and you run into that building." And I would say it about like that, flatly, so I was simply stating the job to be done.

'I remember about the only time I ever gave them any *real* instructions was when they were supposed to rape Diane Ladd. Diane was a young Method actress up from New York and I didn't know exactly how to set this up. So I thought, I'll shoot the rehearsal, which I almost never do, and see what happens. And so they came running into the shot and started ripping at Diane's blouse. I am just the director, but it seems to me that if I were going to be raping a woman, I would not be pulling at her blouse, I would be pulling at her pants. And Diane, the dedicated Method actress that she was, said, "Roger's right, fellas. That's what you should be doing." And they said, yeah, well, okay, all right, and I said, "Right. Now let's do it again." And we did it again and they got it right.'

It was Corman's toughest shoot. 'Roger was tired and frantic by the end,' recalled Bogdanovich, 'That's why the Angels didn't always like Roger: he was an authority figure.'

The travails of *The Wild Angels* did not end with its completion. When it was chosen as the sole American entry and shown on the opening night of the 1966 Venice Film Festival, the State Department, appalled by the violence and by the nihilistic image of the United States it portrayed, tried – and failed – to have the invitation withdrawn. The San Bernadino chapter of the Hell's Angels sued Corman and AIP for defamation, claiming they were portrayed as anti-social outlaws instead of 'a social organisation dedicated to the spreading of technical information on motorcycles'. The action, reportedly for $4 million, failed.

Much of the initial critical reception was hostile as well. However, and certainly not for the first time, the critics proved to be monumentally wrong, and over the ensuing years hindsight-driven rewriting prevailed as various critics attempted to correct their unfortunate original misjudgements as to the significance of *The Wild Angels*.

The public, as always, were ahead of the game (the arrest, trial and acquittal of Peter Fonda for the possession of marijuana and the concomitant publicity did no harm in helping to publicize the picture) and it finally grossed more than $25 million on a budget of some $350,000.

The Wild Angels was banned in Great Britain after it had been screened at the Edinburgh Film Festival. Said Sam Arkoff, 'I find it so offensive that something like this could happen in a country with such a rich history of freedom. You English should not tolerate it.' (Sadly there is no record of how a Scottish audience, however receptive, took to being described as 'English'.)

Story

A Hell's Angel, shot while trying to steal a Highway Patrol motorcycle, is taken from hospital by fellow gang members who rape a nurse in the process. When he dies, they invade a church and hold a funeral service which turns into an orgy before they violently confront locals at the cemetery.

Corman's documentary style direction adds to the impact of a brutal, compelling and ultimately nihilistic melodrama that served as the template/yardstick for the spate of Sixties biker films. It still commands attention. Corman cannily combines unshocked observation with sure-fire exploitation elements to paint a vivid and decidedly unappetising picture of the period and his fast-paced handling compensates for, in particular, Nancy Sinatra who, cast for box-office appeal on the strength of her popularity as a singer, proved to be no actress.

Reviews

'Realistic leather jacket delinquency yarn with plenty of shock value. Strong reception seen in exploitation market. For thematic motivation, Corman, who produces in almost documentary style, has chosen a subject frequently in the headlines ... pinpointed here, the Angels, in vicious stride and without regard for law and order, operate in a Southern California beach community recognised as Venice, and it is upon this particular seg-

ment that Corman directs his clinical eye in dissecting their philosophical (?) rebellion. While not new in tone, treatment is sufficiently compelling to warrant strong exploitation. The Charles B Griffith screenplay carries shock impact of the sort that occasionally stuns. As such, [the] market is somewhat reduced. It is suitable mainly for the exploitation trade and situations which relish their action raw and violent, but lush take is nonetheless indicated. Corman has developed his topic carefully and with an eye to values which pay off in sustained interest. He tackles the assignment with enthusiasm, taking apart the cult and giving its members an in-depth study as he follows a gang headed by Peter Fonda in their defiance of common decencies. Added shock occurs in script focusing on black-jackets staging an orgy in a church after reducing it to a shambles when the minister tries to conduct funeral services for one of their members, and their lugging a body for burial in a cemetery where they start a free-for-all with the townspeople...
Corman's direction carries conviction and he has the benefit of some exceptionally good technical assistance. Outstanding here is Richard Moore's colour camera-work, catching some particularly interesting desert and outdoor backgrounds; Monty Hellman's tight editing; Mike Curb's music score.'
Variety

'Corman's Angels neither perceive that in their cult of violence and terror, in their persecution of minorities, even in their equipment, they emulate their chosen enemies, authority and the police; know that in their unreflective acts of destruction they create the sources of their own as well as other people's suffering ... Corman's achievement in *The Wild Angels* is that he makes this absence of alternatives palpably present. The film's perspective encompasses neither more individual nor more socially acceptable types of revolt, while the few representatives of alternative life-styles (the policeman, the nurse, the minister of religion) are shown to be as trapped within their uniforms and their preconceived ideas as the cyclists are within the set phrases of their imprecise 'cool' language ... Corman's treatment of his subject: the frightening reality of ritualized behaviour'.
Monthly Film Bulletin

'True 'horror' of contemporary society is displayed in this Roger Corman film which opened the Venice Film

The Wild Angels
Hells Angels have come to town: the film starred Peter Fonda, Nancy Sinatra and Bruce Dern

Festival. Vibrant, slick and exciting; a few corny moments, but without Corman the film would have been terrible. Inadequate performance by Nancy Sinatra who should have stayed in a recording studio.'
Castle of Frankenstein

'It's quite possible to dismiss *The Wild Angels* as a thrill-picture about motorcycle hoodlums; no more than a sick, nicely-calculated exploitation film which trades on the fascination which screen violence holds for a large percentage of today's audiences … There's no plot, just a series of situations … But there's no attempt to elicit sympathy or understanding for the Angels, no comforting explanation that they came from broken homes, that their parents were too rich or too poor… in fact, there's nothing to indicate their background at all… Viewed today… *The Wild Angels* (made in 1966) seems almost prophetic; anticipating rather than exploiting an established trend. It would be wrong to read social messages into Corman's film, however. Nobody should mistake him for a moralist. For one reason his work is too sophisticated… Even its detractors wouldn't deny that *The Wild Angels* depicts a descent into hell and spiritual chaos with frightening power… It's a film which has met with a great deal of opposition – from both censors and critics. But as a key work in the Corman canon – and as a startling but unexaggerated picture of contemporary rebellion – it merits attention.'
Films and Filming (July 1969)

'This is the brutal little picture that was shown at the Venice Film festival as an American entry (by invitation) and caused a few diplomats to mop their bows. It is an embarrassment all right – a vicious account of the boozing, fighting, pot-smoking, vandalizing and raping done by a gang of sickle riders who are obviously drawn to represent the swastika-wearing Hell's Angels, one of several disreputable gangs on the West Coast… Mr Corman shot the whole thing in colour and in a *cinema vérité* style that makes it resemble a documentary.'
The New York Times

'Ugly piece of trash.'
Newsweek

CREDITS

The Wild Angels (US 1966)
pc AIP. A Roger Corman Production
assoc p Laurence Cruickshank
ph Richard Moore
ed Monty Hellman
m Mike Curb
90 mins.
p, d Roger Corman
w Charles B Griffith
colour. Panavision
p design Rick Beck-Meyer
mu Jack Obringer

Cast: Peter Fonda (Heavenly Blues), Nancy Sinatra (Mike), Bruce Dern (Loser), Lou Procopio (Joint), Coby Denton (Bull Puckey), Marc Cavell (Frankenstein), Buck Taylor (Dear John), Norm Alden (Medic), Michael J Pollard (Pigmy), Diane Ladd (Gaysh), Joan Shawlee (Momma Monahan), Gayle Hunnicutt (Suzie), Art Baker (Thomas), Frank Maxwell (Preacher), Frank Gerstle (Hospital Policeman), Kim Hamilton (Nurse), Peter Bogdanovich and members of the Hell's Angels, Venice, California.

THE ST VALENTINE DAY'S MASSACRE

'Socko production, direction, scripting. Exploitation bonanza.'

Having made another fortune for AIP with *The Wild Angels*, Corman decided to forget the traumas of his sterile time with Columbia and have another stab at working within the creative constraints of a major studio. He returned to the gangster genre for the first time since *Machine Gun Kelly* almost a decade previously to make *The St Valentine Day's Massacre*. The $1 million provided by Twentieth Century-Fox was his biggest budget to date.

'Corman's films are intended for mass audiences – and too many people still treat with suspicion directors who attempt significant works of art within the framework of a commercial film.'
Films and Filming

Backstory

When I asked him about his time at Fox, Corman told me: 'I enjoyed it reasonably well', but added: 'I didn't get the exact cast I wanted. As a matter of fact, I still remember what happened. I wanted Orson Welles for Al Capone and Jason Robards for Bugs Moran. The studio considered it and they finally said "Orson Welles has given trouble as an actor on every picture you are aware of. This is your first big budget film" – *actually, it was the lowest budget film they made all year.* "We just don't think you should take a chance on Orson disrupting the picture. And he probably isn't going to want to play Al Capone anyway."

'So I switched Jason to the Capone character. He had already accepted the Bugs Moran character and I cast Ralph Meeker as Moran. I think the picture turned out well, but I think it would have been a stronger film if Jason, who really fitted Bugs Moran had played him and Welles had played Capone.

'I was later talking with Welles with Peter Bogdanovich and I asked him what would have happened. He said "I would have loved to have played Capone." Of course, that could have just been casual talk, but I think he would have.'

The St Valentine's Day Massacre not only boasted Corman's biggest budget but also, at 35 days, his longest shooting schedule. He made the most of both and reused standing sets from other Fox pictures: art directors Jack Martin Smith and Philip Jefferies turned a bar from *The Sand Pebbles* into the bar of a Chicago brothel, the manor from *The Sound of Music* was given a new lease of life as Capone's mansion and the huge *Hello, Dolly* exterior sets were given one of the first of their many make-overs and turned up as Twenties Chicago.

Corman found roles for 'repertory player' Barboura Morris and offered Jack Nicholson the role of Johnny May. It was finally played by Bruce Dern after Nicholson turned it down. He was quoted as telling him, 'Roger, I'll be honest with you. I don't want do do the lead. (sic). Do me a favour – give me the smallest part with the longest run you can in the picture.' Corman obliged.

Nicholson's minor part as a driver earned him the most money he had ever been paid on a Corman picture. He relished his one line of dialogue, 'It's garlic – if the bullets don't kill ya, ya die of blood poisoning', which he delivered to reveal what exactly he was using to give his bullets extra impact.

Story

Rivalry between gang leaders Al Capone and Bugs Moran culminates in the bloody massacre of seven of Moran's men by Capone's hoods in a garage in Chicago on 14 February, 1929.

Corman does an exemplary job of illuminating the intricate machinations leading up to the climactic slaying, he potentiates the force of the frequently violent drama with a highly effective, cool, semi-documentary approach to often lurid material and the period is very well evoked. However, the regrettable miscasting of Jason Robards who mistakes over-acting for *good* acting is a major demerit: otherwise, the casting is impeccable, and Corman elicits notable performances from George Segal as killer Peter Gusenberg and Ralph Meeker as Moran. One of the finest genre films in the canon.

Reviews

'Excellent semi-documentary about the 1929 gangland shoot-out. Jason Robards heads solid cast. Socko production, direction, scripting. Exploitation bonanza. Producer-director Roger Corman has come up with a slam-bang, gutsy recreation of 'The St Valentine's Day Massacres', a 1929 gangland sensation of Chicago. Well-written, and presented in semi-documentary style... salty dialogue and violence are motivated properly, and solid production values recreate a bygone era. Torrid b.o. potential evident... treatment permits a hard exploitation sell, but in certain markets an emphasis on the timeless sociological aspects of organized crime might be effective... recurring use of ethnic vulgarisms, today frowned upon, is perfect in context. Frequent gun deals – expertly staged by Corman and edited in terrif fashion by William B Murphy – hold strong interest in the way that people cannot help being both repelled and attracted by disaster and atrocity. While both violence and dialogue make the pic a doubtful item for the very young, such elements are motivated properly in the dramatic sense, thereby escaping any charge of cheap exploitation of brutality for its own sake. Under Corman's excellent direction, entire cast delivers on-target performance.'
Variety

'This is Roger Corman's first (comparatively) big budget film, with major studio trimmings and some splendidly reconstructed settings, and if one feels some slight sense of disappointment it is probably because, given a subject which would seem tailor-made for him, he has – with one exception – made no effort to impose on it his characteristic view of life as a giant horror film. The exception is the superb rose-tinted flashback of the murder of Hymie Weiss... one does detect a slight over-

all flatness, as though Corman had been prevented by the framework from setting his personal seal to the subject. Sequence by sequence, however, there is little to complain about... As a marginal note: Corman is much more successful than Hitchcock was in *The Torn Curtain* (sic) 'in suggesting the *difficulty* of killing – his gangsters dispense carloads of machine-gun bullets, yet only occasionally manage to hit someone.'
Monthly Film Bulletin

'In this reconstruction of gang warfare in Chicago in the late twenties, director Corman has had an eye for detail and succeeds in establishing a period atmosphere which is let down to some extent by some less-than-convincing studio street sets. The action scenes, which are mainly a matter of a hail of machine-gun bullets, are tremendous and quite chilling in the coldboodedness, and the picture rates among the most violent of gangster movies. Characters are many, too many perhaps for an audience to take in. Though each is introduced and commented on in factual style by a commentator, it is sometimes difficult to remember who belongs to which gang. It could be thought that Jason Robards somewhat overplays the admittedly larger-than-life figure of Capone, and some of the acting in the smaller parts is faintly hammy, but on the whole this depiction of the events which culminated in the famous gangland massacre is efficiently done.'
CEA Film Report

'The only plausible reason for *The St Valentine's Day Massacre* that I can see is that is offered its maker, Roger Corman, an opportunity to put on screen an elaborately detailed re-enactment in colour of the famous slaughter of seven members of a Chicago gang. It is not a good gangster picture in any sense of the word. It isn't well constructed, well directed or well played. It is sloppily overwritten and quite excessively performed ... no, the only theatrical value and commercial purpose of this luridly publicized picture... appear to me to be the callous horror and morbid fascination of the terminal scene... For those who like blood and twitching bodies, there is plenty of that in this scene. Mr Corman previously made such warm-up pictures as *Masque of the Red Death* and *Buckets* [sic] *of Blood*.'
The New York Times

'Written by Howard Browne, who is said to be an authority on the Chicago of the '20s, and produced and directed by Roger Corman, who has made a fortune out of sociopathic 'horror' films, this version of the events leading up to the St Valentine's Day Massacre... is superficial sensationalizing. It will hold the interest of those who have never heard of the Capone-Moran feud, but not the interest of those who know something about the role of organized crime in Illinois politics.'
Films in Review

'If there has been a question as to whether or not Roger Corman knows how to spend money, this picture answers the question and the answer is "yes".'
Sight and Sound

'A cool, violent film, romantic in a disciplined, enchanted way about its battling gangsters.'
Spectator

'A well made reconstruction of the bootleg 1930s... can be recommended to those who enjoy a particularly gruesome thriller.'
The People

CREDITS ►►►►►►►►►►►►►

The St Valentine's Day Massacre (US 1967)
pc Los Altos/20th Century-Fox **p, d** Roger Corman
assoc p Paul Rapp   **w** Howard Browne
ph Milton Krasner   **colour**
sp ph fx L B Abbott, Art Cruikshank, Emil Kosa Jr. Panavision
ed William B Murphy   **ad** Jack Martin Smith, Philip Jefferies
m Fred Steiner   **md** Lionel Newman
mu Ben Nye   100 mins.
Cast: Jason Robards (Al Capone), George Segal (Peter Gusenberg), Ralph Meeker (George 'Bugs' Moran), Jean Hale (Myrtle Nelson), Clint Ritchie (Machine Gun Jack McGurn), Frank Silvera (Nicholas Sorello), Joseph Campanella (Al Wienshank), Richard Bakalyan (John Scalisi), David Canary (Frank Gusenberg), Bruce Dern (Johnny May), Harold J Stone (Frank Nitti), Kurt Kreuger (James Clark), Paul Richards (Charles Fischetti), Joseph Turkel (Jack Guzik), Milton Frome (Adam Heyer), Mickey Deems (Reinhart Schwimmer), John Agar (Dion O'Banion), Celia Lovsky (Josephine Schwimmer), Tom Reese (Ted Newberry), Jan Merlin (Willie Marks), Alex D'Arcy (Hymie Weiss), Gus Trikonis (Rio), Charles Dierkop (Salvanti), Tom Signorelli (Bobo Borotto), Rico Cattani (Albert Anselmi), Alex Rocco (Diamond), Leo Gordon (James Morton), Barboura Morris (Jeanette Landsman), Mary Grace Canfield (Mrs Doody), Ron Gans (Chapman), Jack Del Rio, Phil Haran, Nob Brandin, Ernesto Moralli, Nick Norgani (Capone's Board Members), Ken Scott (Policeman), Joan Shawlee (Edna [Frank's girlfriend]), Jack Nicholson (Gino), Paul Frees (Narrator)

'An attempt at a psychedelic experience through film.'

After sampling the mixed delights of big studio, big budget filmmaking, Corman returned to the relative freedom of independent production with *The Trip*. It turned out to be even more controversial than *The Wild Angels* and came under critical attack as the first mainstream American film to deal with the contemporary American drug culture. It was also shown to acclaim at the Cannes Film Festival.

It repeats a theme that's in many of my pictures; that is, if we continue doing what we're doing, we're going to destroy our only hope.
Roger Corman

Backstory

Towards the end of the Sixties, the hippy drug culture was in full swing and had become very much an integral part of the American way of life among young anti-Establishment rebels (as well as the not so young) who were being exhorted by professor Timothy Leary to, 'Tune in, turn in and drop out.' Tripping on LSD became almost *de rigeur* among more trendy substance users, with Leary usefully providing a veneer of intellectual purpose by claiming that 'The aim of all Eastern religion, like the aim of LSD, is basically to get high. That is, to expand your consciousness and find ecstasy within.'

Corman who was ahead of the game as usual and commercially aware of the millions of Americans who were currently seeking their own particular versions of ecstasy through drugs held discussions with James Nicholson and settled on an LSD trip as the subject of his next AIP picture. Charles Griffith spent three months on the project but his two screenplays proved to be unsatisfactory.

Instead Corman went with a script by Jack Nicholson

who had previously written two Westerns (*Flight to Fury* [1966], *Ride in the Whirlwind* [1967]) he had bankrolled. Additionally Corman knew that Nicholson had experimented with LSD. 'I was,' Nicholson told *Playboy*, 'one of the first people in the country to take acid. It was in laboratory conditions on the West Coast.'

Corman felt that he, too, might well benefit from personal experience and decided to drop acid as part of his preparations for directing *The Trip*. 'I took it myself', he told me, 'so I would understand what I was doing. And it became immediately aware to me, immediately obvious to me that there was no way we could reproduce an LSD trip on film, it is so complex. But I evolved the style of shooting and cutting for those sequences which was with the music, which was the closest I could come.'

Corman went with a group of friends and colleagues, including Griffith and his story editor and assistant Frances Doel to drop acid at Big Sur. It took some time for the LSD, which he ingested in a lump of sugar, to take effect after which, Corman later recalled, 'I spent the next seven hours face down in the ground, beneath a tree, not moving, absorbed in the most wonderful trip imaginable. Among other things, I was sure I have invented an utterly new art form. This new art form was the very act of thinking and creating, and you didn't need books or film or music to communicate it: anyone who wanted to experience it would simply lie face down on the ground anywhere in the world and the work of art would be transmitted through the earth from the mind of its creator into the mind of the audience.'

When it came to making the movie, however, Corman sensibly took a more pragmatic approach to his material. His trip had been memorably good. But he also wanted to show that there was a downside to drugs too and that not all trips were good. He was concerned to ensure that *The Trip* did not simply come across uncritically in favour of LSD.

Among other sources, he raided his own Poe films for some highly potent imagery, most notably in the eerie sequence where Peter Fonda hangs upside down menaced by hooded torturers in the kind of subterranean cobweb-cluttered dungeon in which Vincent Price would have felt perfectly at home, and he wittily 'quoted' from other filmmakers like Fellini so that on one level *The Trip* became something of a cineaste's treasury. Noted *Time*: 'In a flurry of flesh, mattresses, flashing lights and kaleidoscopic patterns, an alert viewer will spot some fancy business from such classics as *The Seventh Seal*, *Lawrence of Arabia*, even *The Wizard of Oz*.'

Corman upset Nicholson by casting Bruce Dern as Fonda's friend and drugs mentor, a role he had written for himself. After Nicholson's overlong screenplay had been reduced to manageable proportions, Corman shot for three weeks, filming the medieval flashbacks around Big Sur and giving director-to-be Dennis Hopper a break by getting him to shoot silent second-unit footage in the desert with Fonda.

During a semi-improvised dope-smoking sequence, sound man Phil Mitchell complained that Hopper had used the word 'man' 36 times in a single speech. 'Great', said the director. 'Print it, man.'

Corman had deliberately structured the climax so that it was open-ended. Fonda appears to have returned to 'normal' after his trip, leaving the audience to decide for themselves whether drugs were 'good' or 'bad'.

However, while he was in Europe working on another picture, AIP decided to preface the picture with witless disclaimers and, more destructively, they unilaterally altered Corman's smooth final sequence by breaking it up with a series of rapid cuts and then optically superimposing a shot of cracked glass over Fonda's face so as to imply that LSD had failed to provide any genuine solution to his problems.

Said Sam Arkoff: 'Roger says he didn't like our final edit on *The Trip*. Well, he didn't do the final edit because, at the time, he would be doing three or four movies simultaneously, and he didn't have time to edit it. ...We had an ending where Peter Fonda wakes up, and there's a broken glass effect. Roger didn't like that. He wanted it to be more pro-drug.'

Naturally, there was nothing in the archetypal hyperbolic AIP pressbook for the film to indicate that there had been any behind-the-scenes traumas. Corman was quoted as saying: 'Although we will not attempt to delve into the pros and cons of LSD in *The Trip*, we will provide the audience with more experience than anyone has dared to show on the subject. Then if anyone wishes to make a judgement on LSD they'll have something on which to base their decision. What we will show is life, even though to some it will be unreal, to others unbelievable *and to a vocal few without excuse*.'

In this latter aspect (my italics) the publicists proved to be unusually prescient. *The Trip* was the first mainstream Hollywood movie about drug use. It was acclaimed at the Cannes Film Festival and audiences voted for it at the box-office, making it a major moneyspinner for AIP, earning them over $6 million. But its release also caused a predictable media storm with Catholic organisations and other conservative pressure groups who condemned what they saw as 'reprehensible' characterisation of its anti-social anti-heroes.

Many film critics also objected to the film, with Judith Crist summarizing *The Trip* on television as 'an hour and a half commercial for LSD'. Possibly she achieved some kind of catharsis by publicly stating her simplistic views but the real effect of her comments was almost certainly to encourage even more people to see the film.

In 1995, the enormous change in attitudes towards drugs that had taken place over the previous three decades enabled Corman to re-categorise his film neatly in line with Nineties Green preoccupations when he said: 'I did a picture called *The Trip* in the sixties with Peter Fonda and Dennis Hopper that made some ecological points through an LSD trip'. Unsurprisingly, this particular aspect of the film had been completely missed by commentators at the time of its initial release. (In Britain, in fact, it was predictably refused a certificate by the Censor and only emerged several years later when, still uncertificated, it was shown at the members-only New Cinema Club in London).

Story

A television commercials director elects to drop acid in the hope that it will provide the self-knowledge he needs to sort out his fractured personal relationships and his unsatisfactory professional life.

While Corman imaginatively deploys Arch Dalzell's fluid colour cinematography, some (relatively) inexpensive in-camera special effects and sharp-edged editing, the film is rather more satisfying visually than as a dramatic examination of the Sixties drug culture and it now comes over as very much a period piece and needs to be viewed as such. Nevertheless, in spite of obvious budgetary constraints, the key hallucinatory sequences and, in particular, the bravura psychedelic nightclub scene are remarkably effective. Fonda's hippie image makes him ideal casting for the role and gives his performance a useful added dimension, while Dern is outstanding. In the final analysis, the combination of Corman's assured creative and filmmaking skills, the potent blend of sex, drugs and a superb musical score by The American Flag serve to confirm *The Trip* as the quintessential Sixties drug movie.

Reviews

'An attempt at a psychedelic experience through film, [the] pic depends mostly on editing gimmicks and cross cutting, but should do boffo box-office biz with the youth market. As a far-out free floating LSD freak-out, *The Trip* should provide enough psychedelic jolts, sexsational scenes and mind-blowing montages and optical effects for the youth market. No story line in the conventional sense; pic mainly depends on cinematic gimmicks to grab the viewers attention and so dabbles in Bergman and Fellini symbols and techniques. Main problem in viewing *The Trip* is trying to guess the intent. Is producer-director Roger Corman simply exploiting a new horror avenue or is this an honest attempt to reproduce by film an actual hallucinatory experience?'
Variety

'Reproduces the sensations of an LSD trip with remarkable accuracy (sic). It vividly recreates the visual distortions, the rapid, often subliminal cutting from image to image and the swirling, kaleidoscopic colour patterns: the 'pretty pictures', the upper strata of the LSD effect. More importantly, Corman also conveys the deeper psychic levels which are opened out under the drug... Technically, the film is a dazzling and brilliant work, Corman bringing off the stunning effects with a skill

acters are forever entombed in the labyrinth of their unconscious minds, symbolised in the Poe cycle by those haunted, cobwebbed Gothic mansions. They never attain the salvation which comes from reconciling self-destructive and irrational impulses.'
Films and Filming (June 1969)

'To see it today, five years too late, is something of an oddity. It is so innocent, so earnest, so well meaning and, of course, so naive. Naturally it has very little to do with an actual LSD experience, but it does give you a look into the heads of Corman and Nicholson – the former is not unnaturally hung up on a lot of Hammer, American International, symbolic Poe, while Jack's five easy pieces all had big tits and hips ... For the first 15 minutes or so of *The Trip*, it is, in its own words, 'into some really beautiful stuff'. but it can't possible sustain an hour and a half of it... Pure innocence tinged with psychedelic boredom.'
Films and Filming (1971)

'A psychedelic tour through the bent mind of Peter Fonda, which is evidently full of old movies. ...the photographer's camera work is bright enough and full of tricks, without beginning to suggest the heightened inner awareness so frequently claimed by those who use the drug.'
Time

'The subject matter of *The Trip* enables the director to make a totally incoherent movie with erratic, repetitious and fake-arty effects that simply nauseate, both intellectually and physically. This is one trip to skip.'
NBC Today Show (Judith Crist)

'If *The Trip* is a fair indication of what one sees when high on psychedelic drugs, take it from me the experience is not very different from looking at some of the phantasmagoric effects in movies like *Juliet of the Spirits*. In trying to visualize a notion of what Peter Fonda goes through... Roger Corman has simply resorted to a long succession of familiar cinematic images, accompanied by weird music and sounds... Is this a psychedelic experience? Is this what it's like to take a trip? If it is, then it's

warn you that all you are likely to take away... is a painful case of eye-strain and perhaps a detached retina.'
The New York Times

'Corman holds attention with imaginative special effects that eventually knock your eyes out. He overdoes quick-cutting action sequences, especially in the last third of the film... the result is more a camera happening in an unreal world than the commentary it supposedly sets out to be. Motives for theme and treatment are open to debate... Its inconclusive ending is likely to leave viewers asking: '"Was this trip necessary?"'
New York Daily News

'The *8 1/2* of exploitation films! Roger Corman's personal exploration of hallucinogenic drug experience owes less to Leary than Fellini. Some arresting effects in plotless recreation of some of Corman's own 'trip', loaded with references to his earlier work, snippets of Bergmanesque imagery, rapid editing, eye-splitting visuals, and some typical Corman gags. Brilliant performance by Bruce Dern. We knew you could do it, Roger!'
Castle of Frankenstein

'If Corman sees LSD as a spiritual confidence trick as blatantly and blandly dishonest as any TV commercial, he also realises that its fancy-free images can have a hallucinating beauty that no TV camera can capture. Reputedly, he tried LSD before making *The Trip*. Whether he did or not is really of no consequence, since the visions are culled from his own treasury of signs and symbols and archetypes, made even more weird and wonderful than before by Arch Dalzell's superb colour photography... all are quintessentially Corman... Corman obviously had himself a ball with the superb, stunningly controlled colour compositions. But if the visions are drawn from Corman's own rich repertoire, their authenticity as an experience is guaranteed by the way he handles his actors... Whether *The Trip* is likely to stimulate drug-taking, as the censor's ban and the panicky disclaimers tacked on at the beginning suggest, seems very arguable. Much less arguable is that this is a brilliant piece of film-making.'
Monthly Film Bulletin

'*The Trip* pulls no punches. This is a smash commercial picture on the national youth problem of taking psychedelic drugs.'
Boxoffice

CREDITS ❯❯❯❯❯❯❯❯❯❯❯❯❯

The Trip (US 1967)
pc AIP. A Roger Corman Production   **p, d** Roger Corman
w Jack Nicholson   **ph** Arch Dalzell
colour   **ed** Ronald Sinclair
pyschedelic sequences Dennis Jakob
pyschedelic fx Peter Gardiner   **cost** Richard Bruno.
m The American Flag, an American band
85 mins.
Cast: Peter Fonda (Paul Groves), Susan Strasberg (Sally), Bruce Dern (John), Dennis Hopper (Max), Salli Sachse (Glenn), Katherine Walsh (Lulu), Barboura Morris (Flo), Caren Bernsen (Alexadra), Dick Miller (Cash), Luana Anders (Waitress), Tommy Signorelli (Al), Mitzi Hoag (Wife), Judy Lang (Nadine), Barbara Renson (Helena), Susan Walters, Frankie Smith (Go-Go Girls)

De Sade
Corman retells the tale of the man who gave us sadism, Keir Dullea as the Marquis with Senta Berger as his wife

Corman took no credit for his directorial contribution to the film that was intended to be one of AIP's biggest Sixties successes. Prior to its release *Variety* wrote that *De Sade* would 'bridge the generation gap. It will attract both the turned-on hip and the dirty old men.' In the event, however, it attracted bad reviews and meagre audiences to match.

I stepped away, Dick Matheson wrote the script, Cy directed it – did a very good job, I think. But it ended up pretty much as what I had said – they couldn't show what they had to show. And therefore the picture was never a completely successful film.
Roger Corman

Backstory

'Actually, I started that project with Dick Matheson' Corman spoke about his brief involvement with *De Sade*. 'Dick worked out the storyline and I liked the way it was told and then I withdrew from the project and I remember the reason. I said to Jim, "I would just like to step away from this. I know I have done some work in preparation but I won't charge you for it. I think I don't want to do the picture and I really think the picture should not be made." And I said, for this reason, and it isn't prudishness on my part.

'"If you are going to make the picture you have to show certain scenes of sadism and you can't show them and have the picture shown. And if you don't show them, you don't have any picture and you are in a no-win situation. I really think this picture should not be made", so they said all right.'

Corman left the project and AIP, who were co-producing the film in Germany with Artur Brauner, hired Cy Endfield, who was then best known for *Zulu*, to direct. But AIP producer Louis Heyward found Endfield was failing to shoot according to the schedule and asked him why. 'He said, "Well I don't want to do the sex scenes now – it's too disruptive",' recalled Heyward, who told him, 'But we're using these sets now. If we don't shoot, we'll have to rewrite the scene.'

'He said, "No, let's pass". So we went on, and then there was another sex scene that went missing. Then another. He was skipping over them all.

'I called Sam [Arkoff] and said, "We're in big trouble". I thought Endfield was getting fatigued, so we took some action.' Endfield went into hospital to get some rest and Corman flew to Germany to take over.

According to Arkoff, Keir Dullea reacted badly to the news of the new director, calling him 'That exploitation director!' Arkoff told him 'the only director I know who can finish this picture quickly is Roger Corman. He can handle it. He can tie loose ends together faster than anyone' and calmed the actor by pointing out that Corman was 'very educated, very intelligent'.

AIP gave *De Sade* a gaudy Hollywood-style premiere at the Rivoli Theatre on Broadway. It was the first such event in the history of the company but it turned out to be money ill spent and it did not help the picture gain a good reception.

Story

Alleged biopic of the Marquis de Sade.

Unfortunate and near-unwatchable.

Reviews

'A gloomy and dreary affair. The story is confusing and impossible to follow and one is left wondering which events were fantasy and reality. There is a fair amount of nudity and a few sex orgies but cuts are obvious throughout (in America the running time was 120 mins.). A lavish production as regards costumes and sets, the film mainly consists of dialogue and moves at a pedestrian pace with very little action to liven things up. The whole thing makes weird entertainment and has little to offer popular audiences; some will be attracted to its title but are likely to be disappointed with the result.'
CEA Film Report

'AIP's highly touted "biggest production to date" mixes silly sex, teasing, obfuscating symbolism and surprisingly low-grade production in tortuous *Citizen Kane*-inspired version of De Sade's life and crimes. Promising approach, inane results... Dir. Cy Endfield, with an uncredited (thankfully) assist from Roger Corman.'
Castle of Frankenstein

'Symbol and character, mood and meaning never cohere closely enough to avoid a suggestion, at the unhappiest moments, of a *Fall of the House of Usher* mislocated in time and place.'
Monthly Film Bulletin

CREDITS ▶▶▶▶▶▶▶▶▶▶▶▶▶▶

De Sade/Der Marquis de Sade/ Das Ausschweufende de Leben des Marquise de Sade (US/West Germany 1969)
pc AIP/CCC/Transcontinental
exec p Louis M Heyward, Artur Brauner
p Samuel Z Arkoff, James H Nicholson   **assoc p** Pat Green.
d Cy Endfield   **uncredited d** Roger Corman
w Richard Matheson. Peter Berg
From the biography by Gilbert Lely and the correspondence of the Marquis de Sade
ph Heinz Pehlke   **colour**
ed Max Benedict, Hermann Haller   **ad** Jürgen Kiebach
optical fx Cinefx   **cost** Vangie Harrison
m Billy Strange   **titles** Sandy Dvore
113 mins.
Cast: Keir Dullea (Marquis de Sade), Senta Berger (Anne de Sade), Lilli Palmer (Madame de Montreuil), John Huston (Abbé de Sade), Anna Massey (Renée de Montreuil), Uta Levka (Rose Keller), Herbert Weissbach (M d Montreuil), Christiane Krüger (De Sade's Mistres), Sonja Zienann (Le Beauvoisin), Max Kiebach (de Sade as a boy)

TARGET: HARRY

'Corman oldie finally hits the screen.'

I had never been to Istanbul. I thought I would like to shoot a picture there, so I came up with a story that enabled me to shoot the climax of What's in it For Harry? *in Istanbul.*
Roger Corman

In 1969 Corman directed his first made-for-television movie. It was intended to be the pilot for a proposed action series: the series never happened and, in the event, *Target: Harry* was not shown in the United States until over a decade later, and it surfaced only briefly in British cinemas in 1979.

Backstory

'It was a sort of Movie of the Week before there was a Movie of the Week', Corman said. 'I made up the idea as I was going into this meeting with ABC and said to them, "The hero is an anti-hero, he operates out of Tangier and he's a pilot with an old beat-up amphibian plane and he is for hire. He will fly anywhere, do anything that's reasonably legal, somewhere between a mercenary and a private eye and an adventurer for hire. He can go any place, do anything, he wears an old leather jacket, and he has got a little bit of a drinking problem." 'They said yes, they said they would think about it, but they thought they would do it. I had a film at the Venice Film Festival and they called me there and said "We're going to go ahead with it. On your way back, go to Tangier and scout the locations." I did, and I found some great locations.

'When I came back to Hollywood, they said "Everything is fine, we are going ahead, but we have done some research and we're going to make a few changes. We are going to move the locale from Tangier to Monte Carlo and we don't think the old dirty bomber jacket is right. We see him in a blue blazer and a little more sophisticated. And as for the idea that he has a drinking problem, we think it would be nice if he had a Martini – occasionally."

'I shot the film, I did the best I could, we had a great time. We shot all over Monte Carlo, in Turkey, everywhere – but the concept did undergo some major changes.'

Given *Target Harry*'s minor, atypical place in the Corman canon, it is perhaps appropriate that he billed himself as 'Henry Neill'.

Story

An adventurer, hired in Monte Carlo to fly a thief to Istanbul with printing plates stolen from London's Royal Mint, is caught up in intrigue, mystery and murder.

The Maltese Falcon meets James Bond: while the locations are better than either the story or the acting, there is plenty of fast-moving action and it does not take itself seriously. Director Monte Hellman served as editor and long-time Corman repertory member Beech Dickerson (*Rock All Night*, *Attack of the Crab Monsters*, *War of the Satellites*, *Teenage Caveman*, etc) was assistant director.

Reviews

'Corman oldie finally hits the screen. 'Film is more interesting historically than for its intrinsic merits, as it was one of Roger Corman's last helming jobs before abandoning the helmer's chair for the executive suite in 1971. Produced by Gene Corman in the late 1960s for ABC, the film was reportedly deemed too violent for the tube by the network. With a couple of nude scenes added it was later advertised in trade ads as *How to Make It*, but evidently never saw the light of day, at least domestically. One Henry Neill receives on-screen directing credit, but the appearance of Roger Corman in a couple of shots, along with reliable accounts by his collaborators, certifies his involvement with the project ... mild suspenser... done on the cheap with natural sets and locations. Film is routine but competent on every level and would have served satisfactorily as a tv pic.'
Variety (26.3.1980)

'A fairly minor item in the Corman Company's repertoire... the tone wavers uncertainly between tongue-in-cheek pastiche and straight, thick-ear thriller, with the obvious plotting making the discrepancy all the more obvious.'
Monthly Film Bulletin

TH-3

CREDITS ⪢⪢⪢⪢⪢⪢⪢⪢⪢

Target: Harry/What's In It For Harry/(TVT)/ How To Make It (US 1969)

pc The Corman Company. For ABC Pictures International

p Gene Corman

d Roger Corman (as 'Henry Neill')

ph Patrice Pouget

ed Monte Hellman

cost Carolyn Diliberto

mu Nicole Barbe

81 mins

assoc p Charles Hannawalt

w Bob Barbash

colour

p design Sharon Compton

m Les Baxter

stunt co-ordinator Earl Parker

Cast: Vic Morrow (Harry Black), Suzanne Pleshette (Diane Reed), Victor Buono (Mosul Rashi), Cesar Romero (Lieutenant George Duval), Stanley Holloway (Jason Carlyle), Charlotte Rampling (Ruth Carlyle), Michael Ansara (Major Milos Segora), Katy Fraysse (Lisa Boulez), Christian Barber ('Bulley' Boulez), Fikret Hakan (Inspector Devrim), Milton Reid (Kemal), Anna Capri (Francesca), Laurie Main (Simon Scott), Victoria Hale (Michele), Jack Leonard (Valdez), Roger Corman (Man on Telephone)

BLOODY MAMA

'Abundant violence and sex.'

In the wake of Arthur Penn's successful, groundbreaking (at least in terms of mainstream violence) but critically overrated period piece *Bonnie and Clyde*, Corman returned to gangster movies with an even bloodier biopic, *Bloody Mama*, which turned out to be his penultimate picture for AIP. It remains one of his favourite films.

'The family that **slays** *together stays together …You gotta believe … you gotta have faith … but first you gotta get rid of the witnesses!'*
Promotion for *Bloody Mama*

Backstory

By the end of the Sixties, Shelley Winters was heading inexorably towards larger-than-life, frequently grotesque character roles in star-driven shockers, following the example of Bette Davis and Joan Crawford who had had an unexpected hit with *Whatever Happened to Baby Jane*.

Before Winters joined in exploitation circles with horror movies like *What's the Matter With Helen?* and *Who Slew Auntie Roo?*, Corman elicited a bravura tour de force from her as the infamous Kate 'Ma' Barker who led her murderous sons on a bloody reign of terror in the Ozarks during the Thirties Depression. (Winters had already played the character in *The Biggest Mother of the Them All* episode of the *Batman* television series in 1966.)

Corman chose *Bloody Mama* from a number of scripts

AIP offered him and reworked Robert Thom's screenplay to his satisfaction with another writer. Corman put the film into production after a short hiatus occasioned by the assassinations of Bobby Kennedy and Martin Luther King: it was felt that filming an ultra-violent movie might be inappropriate right then. The hiatus soon passed.

Winters, as had happened the previous year when she made *Wild in the Streets* for AIP, wanted to rewrite not just her own role but those of other actors as well. AIP held out against these creative demands but Corman allowed her to have some input on casting, and Winters put up Robert De Niro to play her sadistic junkie son Lloyd.

Corman agreed and gave the actor his first major role. 'I had no problem with casting him because I had seen the films he had done with Brian De Palma by this stage', said Corman, 'and again they impressed me with his level of concentration and the way he seemed to be totally into the work.' Corman's acting classes stood him in excellent stead now since his key players, like him, were grounded in Method acting.

De Niro, in particular, immersed himself in his role, leaving early for the Arkansas locations to learn the local accent: he was so successful that he was able to double as a dialogue coach. He also decided he needed to lose weight to play Lloyd Barker and worried Corman and his co-stars when he shed some 30 pounds during filming to achieve the emaciated look of a dying drug addict.

Corman took only four weeks to shoot the film on location in the Ozarks in northern Arkansas, coping with potential disasters like De Niro taking a wild ride in a period car and only admitting afterwards that he did not know how to drive and was simply 'acting' at being a driver – proof perhaps that there was Method in his madness.

Corman contended impressively, too, with some potentially unnerving behaviour by Winters who, on one occasion, spent the night keeping company with a coffin in a funeral parlour in order to get into the right mood before she exploded into the hyper-emotional scene for the burial of her son De Niro.

'Roger', approved Winters, 'understood the delicate mechanisms of the actor, of working in Method. Actors liked working with him. Roger did what the great directors all do. He rehearsed quite a bit, then he'd get a take right away. That way, you can't plan anything and you get a spontaneous quality to it.'

Spontaneity was certainly the essence of the scene where, after Winters punched Don Stroud as part of the scripted action, he lost it and, leaving the script behind, hit back and floored Winters. By the time Winters came to ask the fast-shooting Corman whether there would be a retake, the moment – and the set-up – had passed and so Stroud's knock-down remained in the finished film.

Corman's enviable ability to spot future stars was not just limited to actors. He gave John A Alonzo, who up to then had been photographing documentaries, his first feature film assignment. 'I was spoiled by Roger and I've made almost 50 movies since then', said Alonzo who went on to shoot *Chinatown* and *Close Encounters of the Third Kind*. 'I though being a d.p. was a piece of cake. He was never intimidating. He'd just look through the lens and say, "That's fine".'

Bloody Mama was a financial success for AIP. However, in common with many other Corman pictures, it was greeted far more positively outside the United States, notably in Europe where there was less snobbish critical hostility towards commercial – as opposed to art – movies.

Story

Kate 'Ma' Barker abandons her weak husband and leads her four sons on a rampage of robbery, murder, rape and kidnapping in the Ozarks during the Depression.

Corman pulls few punches in his savage biopic that is sometimes almost tongue-in-cheek in its excessive portrayal of the 'family that *slays* together stays together'. Excess is the name of the game and they are joined by one son's homosexual lover after he gets out of jail and another's prostitute girlfriend. Incest, drug addiction and other assorted perversions spice the story.

Reviews

'Abundant violence and sex in fair meller about a Depression-era gang. ...Very good b.o. ... a pseudo-biopic starring Shelley Winters in one of those all-over-the-screen performances which sometimes are labelled as bravura acting. Produced and directed by Roger Corman, the film was made entirely on location in Arkansas, and manifests an apparently deliberate attempt at naturalistic filming, including the clumsiness and crudity of documentary film-making ... enough sex and violence to make it a very good commercial bet... Corman's production has the naturalistic look sought, but the occasionally poor looping and uneven colour and textural qualities add up to a liability. His direction is passive, unpretentious and unambitious and therefore nearly non-existent.'
Variety

'Most exhibitors are likely to know this film by reputation as an unusually tough and violent saga of a gangster family. For some time it received no BBFC certificate and seemed unlikely to achieve commercial distribution in this country, but now it is available in a version which is cut, although the pruning has been so cleverly and judiciously done that one is seldom conscious of deletions having been made. The bath murder of a girl and scenes dealing with rape and incest have probably been the most affected, though the movie remains pretty strong fare, quite vicious at times, even though violence is an integral part of the story. Shelley Winters is tremendous in the title role, the general level of acting elsewhere is high, and the picture is imaginatively and stylishly presented.'
CEA Film Report

'He certainly hasn't glamorized them, in the sense that they are not beautiful people like Penn's Bonnie and Clyde, and yet they are undoubtedly romantic creations, viewed through an intense awareness that they were

born on the dark side of the moon of a society which offered them no choice but to live a dead-end existence of one kind or another ... a true film-maker of terror, he sees them as driven by darker, more inexplicable impulses, and doomed to work their own destruction as fanatically as the hapless descendants of the House of Atreus.'
Sight and Sound

'Repulsive, brilliantly unsentimental, occasionally funny.'
The Sunday Times

'Takes the bare bones of *Bonnie and Clyde* but leaves the beauty and the brains behind ... I can understand some people relishing this film: would-be gunslingers for whom the country is insufficiently violent, rural and urban victims of an educational system that enlightens the rich and imprisons the poor ... what I can't understand is how critics who are supposed to know a bit more than the commonest man can discuss such a movie as anything but a shrewd commercial exercise.'
Newsweek

CREDITS >>>>>>>>>>>>>

Bloody Mama (1969)
pc AIP
exec p Samuel Z Arkoff, James H Nicholson
p, d Roger Corman   **co-p** Norman T Herman
w Robert Thom   **st** Robert Thom, Don Peters
ph John A Alonzo   **colour.**
ed Eve Newman   **m** Don Randi
title song Don Randy, Guy Hemric, Bob Silver
sung by Bigfoot   **cost** Thomas Costich
sfx A D Flowers   **mu** David Grayson
90 mins
Cast: Shelley Winters (Kate 'Ma' Barker), Pat Hingle (Sam Adams Pendlebury), Don Stroud (Herman Barker), Diane Varsi (Mona Gibson), Bruce Dern (Kevin Dirkman), Clint Kimbrough (Arthur Barker), Robert De Niro (Lloyd Barker), Robert Walden (Fred Barker), Alex Nicol (George Barker), Michael Fox (Dr Roth), Scatman Crothers (Moses), Stacy Harris (Agent McClellan), Pamela Dunlap (Rembrandt), Lisa Jill (Young Kate), Steve Mitchell (Sheriff), Roy Idom (Ferryboat Passenger)

Bloody Mama
Spawn of the devil. Shelley Winters and her criminal brood

GAS-S-S-S!

With his next film, Corman showed himself to be as unpredictable as ever. He radically changed direction yet again with his strange comic satire *Gas-s-s-s! ... or It May Become Necessary to Destroy the World in Order to Save It.*

The film was intended to tap the still profitable Sixties revolutionary youth market but, for once, Corman's aim was off, and while the film has achieved a certain a cult status with the passage of time, it remains one of his very few pictures that failed to make money.

Its poor reception was made worse by the fact that it was not the film Corman had intended to make. Without consulting him, Sam Arkoff and James Nicholson ruthlessly re-edited the picture in post-production, not to its advantage. As a result *Gas-s-s-s!* marked the termination of Corman's long association with AIP.

When Jim Nicholson and I watched that movie, it gave us gas-s-s-s!
Samuel Z Arkoff

Backstory

Gas-s-s-s!, like AIP's 1968 *Wild in the Streets*, posits a society where there are only young people. This time, however, the brave new world is brought about by accident after an experimental nerve gas that speeds the ageing process is released and it kills everyone over the age of 25.

Corman, who was still working with writer George Armitage when he began the picture in Dallas, regretted going into production without a completed script or adequate preparation.

'If I can teach anybody anything,' he said in London in 1991, 'It would be to have a finished script and adequate preparation. Winter was closing in, and I wanted to shoot the picture before winter, so I shot without enough preparation. I and George Armitage were writing every night on that.'

Corman paid homage to his AIP past by giving Edgar Allan Poe a speaking role. '*Gas-s-s-s!* wasn't that closely related to Poe,' he recalled. 'It was actually a second thought when we put Poe in it. We just started putting things in. In the original concept, he wasn't in it. And we just decided to put him on a motorcycle – it seemed appropriate.'

Gas-s-s-s! was made entirely on location. Armitage accompanied Corman and doubled in front of the cameras as Billy the Kid in addition to his writing chores.

'The *Gas-s-s-s!* shoot was the toughest one I ever saw Roger go through,' said production manager Paul Rapp. Record cold and blizzards marred the start of filming in Dallas at Thanksgiving where Corman restaged the Kennedy assassination.

He then moved west through Texas and New Mexico, rewriting as he went along, shooting his way out of trouble whenever he had to on his way to the final location, the high mesa of the Tacoma Indian Pueblo. When The Grateful Dead asked for more money to appear in the film, Corman economised by replacing them with the less expensive Country Joe and The Fish.

At the Tacoma Pueblo, his budget was further strained when the Indians demanded more money for their services. 'The Indians were terrible to work with,' said

Rapp. 'The last scene was a big action shot with the entire cast, dune buggies, motorcycles and the whole Indian tribe coming together. The first take was a complete mess.' The second take, however, was perfect.

Corman had planned the climax so that God would be heard speaking over the final panning shot. Regrettably, the editors, who re-cut *Gas-s-s-s!* while Corman was in Ireland filming *Von Richthofen and Brown,* decided otherwise, and the voice of God was heard no more in the land in the mutilated AIP release version. Corman was understandably appalled, claiming he had given God, played by Lennie Weinrib, the best lines in the film.

'They took every questionable or controversial point out of the picture; and that was what the picture was all about,' said Corman. 'So it became an extremely innocuous and slightly meaningless picture. And that's what went out. No one ever saw the picture as it was made.'

Arkoff claimed that Corman himself did not particularly like *Gas-s-s-s!*. Corman, who believed that AIP was scared of the film in its original state and thought that they had wrecked it, admitted in 1991, 'I like the film, but it was one I felt didn't really come together.'

Story

After experimental nerve gas from a government research establishment in Alaska accidentally escapes and kills off everyone over age 25, survivors who resent the resumption of political infighting by the young set off for a hippie commune in New Mexico in search of a better life.

Corman uses his picaresque, barely visible storyline to take a series of engaging hit-and-miss satirical sideswipes at various Sixties targets. Some of these – such as the ultra-conservative Hell's Angels who ride golf carts instead of choppers and vigorously protect their country club territory, a fascist team of raping and pillaging footballers and the appearance of such iconic figures as John F Kennedy, Che Guevara and Martin Luther King as bit players – come off splendidly. There is a satisfying amount of comic imagination on display, with the top-hatted, chopper-riding Edgar Allan Poe and his Raven turning up at appropriate points in the narrative to comment on the action. Corman affectionately parodies some of his own films, including *The Trip* and appropriately, *The Raven,* and in spite of its deficiencies, it is

sometimes exhilaratingly surreal (a drive-in cinema is showing the unlikely double bill of *The Sound of Music* and *Ten Days that Shook the World*) and it is never less than interesting, particularly in the context of the Corman canon. However, rather too frequently there is an uncomfortable sense of anything-goes straining for significance, real or imagined, although – given AIP's assault on the film – it is difficult to assess whether these creative lacunae are inherent or the result of crass cutting. Most of the (then) largely unknown cast competently do what is expected of them: Bud Cort, Cindy Williams and Elaine Giftos do rather more.

Reviews

'Aimed at youth but seems way off-target. Producer-director Roger Corman, who has about as good a batting average in the low to medium-budget film as any independent filmmaker, has struck out with this one. An assortment of unproven talent, with the possible exception of the rock group, Country Joe and the Fish, it doesn't seven have the usual fine Corman colour photography and art direction to make it plausible ... Corman, in trying to 'put down' the present way of life has tackled too many targets. Some of them deserve such treatment, others do not. As a result, some comments are funny, many are tasteless ... there's a bit of nudity, despite the GP rating, but it's so poorly photographed and psychedelically lit that it is harmless ... Obviously aimed at the youth market, it will take some very tolerant youngsters to sit through this, poorest of the Corman films.'
Variety

'It is one of the continuing mysteries of this country's distribution system than an inspired piece of lunacy like Roger Corman's *Gas!* takes four years to reach our screens while tripe like *The Red Baron* happily trips across the Atlantic ... the scene seems set for a *Wild in the Streets* youth diatribe, but instead Corman launches into a sustained, 70-minute mick-take of everything from his own films to the Great American Way of Life. *Gas!* has a lightness of touch and controlled wit rarely encountered in US parodies; more importantly, Corman's genuine affection for his targets shines through the barbed jokes, creating exactly the right atmosphere for the unending succession of one- and two-line gags ... *Gas!* is a gigantic dig-in-the-eye for

Gas-s-s-s!
An experimental nerve gas is released. Bruce Karcher as Edgar Allen Poe

those who would glorify Corman's films above their disposable level, a straight two fingers to pretension and phoniness. As such, it is doubly welcome ... *Gas!* is there to be enjoyed – a genuine anarchic comedy devoid of bitterness or politicizing. Above all, it possesses that rare thing: comic invention.'
Films and Filming

'Displaying cheery indifference to its own survival; in fact, *Gas!* self-parodyingly eats itself up as it goes along: this time Corman begins with a holocaust (of a gently euphoric order) and ends on a hallelujah resolution of the forces of good and evil ... *Gas!* has the agreeable distinction of being the one genuine hip allegory of the transformation of Middle America which at the same time manages to send up all other claimants to the title.'
Monthly Film Bulletin

'It's Corman's satirical summing-up of the Sixties.'
Castle of Frankenstein

CREDITS ▶▶▶▶▶▶▶▶▶▶▶▶

Gas-s-s-s, or it Became Necessary to Destroy the World in Order to Save It/Gas-s-s! (US 1969)
(GB: **Gas! or it Became Necessary to Destroy the World in Order to Save It**)

pc San Jacinto. For AIP	**p, d** Roger Corman
assoc p, w George Armitage	**p manager** Paul Rapp
ph Ron Dexter	**colour**
ed George Van Noy	**ad** Dave Nichols
m Country Joe and the Fish	**add m** Barry Melton
79 mins	

Cast: Robert Corff (Coel), Elaine Giftos (Cilla), Pat Patterson (Demeter), George Armitage (Billy the Kid), Alex Wilson (Jason), Alan Braunstein (Dr Drake), Ben Vereen (Carlos), Cindy Williams (Marissa), Bud Cort (Hooper), Talia Coppola (later Talia Shire) (Coralie), Country Joe McDonald (AM Radio), Lou Procopio (Marshall McLuhan), Jackie Farley (Ginnie), Phil Borneo (Quant), David Osterhout (Texas Ranger), Bruce Karcher (Edgar Allan Poe), Mike Castle (Hippie), Jim Etheridge (Renegade cowboy), Peter Fain (Policeman), Stephen Graham (Thief), Bob Easton (Fanatic Religious Leader), Juretta Taylor, Johnny and the Tornados, The Gourmet's Delight

VON RICHTHOFEN AND BROWN

Von Richthofen and Brown
Red Baron (John Phillip Law)

At the time that AIP were unilaterally taking their scissors to *Gas-s-s-s!*, Corman was in Ireland filming *Von Richthofen and Brown*. It turned out to be his last film as director for two decades. In 1970, he married Julie Halloran and went on to establish himself as a major latter-day Hollywood mogul with his hugely successful production-distribution company, New World Pictures and, subsequently, Concorde-New Horizons.

Watching Roger direct is like watching a dance. He has flow and rhythm and concentration.
Julie Corman

Backstory

Corman had long been intrigued by the idea of aristocrats at war, and finally got an opportunity with the story of German World War One air ace Baron Manfred von Richthofen and the Canadian pilot Roy Brown who finally downed him.

After World War One there was no longer a place on the battlefield for 'gentleman warriors' and their now invalid codes of personal honour and chivalry were replaced by the more efficient mass slaughter of twentieth-century mechanised warfare. (The passing of the age of chivalry is vividly exemplified in poignant World War One newsreel footage where mounted officers charge the biplane that is strafing them with raised swords and are cut down by machine gun fire.)

Corman filmed *Von Richthofen and Brown*, produced by his brother Gene, in under six weeks on location in Ireland, for less that $1 million. It emerged looking considerably more expensive, thanks in large measure to the fact that Corman had been able to hire the period aircraft that had been built for *The Blue Max* (1966) and *Darling Lili* (1969) and which were also filmed in Ireland.

Corman took only two weeks to shoot his aerial sequences for which he employed both stunt fliers and members of the Irish Air Force. He filmed simultaneously with three units, one of which was directed by former animator James Murakami who storyboarded aerial sequences and later became one of Corman's directors, most notably on *Battle Beyond the Stars* (1980).

Corman once again demonstrated his mastery of fast, economical movie-making by shooting in every kind of weather on the sensible and historically correct basis that the World War One fliers did not wait around for a perfect day before going into battle.

After completing filming in Ireland and returning to the United States, Corman found he needed more shots of crashing planes and came up with an archetypally (for him) ingenious solution. He found some youngsters who built scale models of World War One aircraft, some of them radio-controlled, which Corman used to stage the action footage he needed at Andrews Air Force Base.

Corman was able to cast *Gas-s-s-s!* screenwriter George Armitage in a small acting role, but United Artists who were financing the picture turned down Bruce Dern who was Corman's original choice for Roy Brown. Don Stroud – whom Corman had selected to play Von Richthofen – was givem the role instead and John Phillip Law was cast as the Baron.

Unfortunately, United Artists' interference did not stop at casting and they insisted, to the film's considerable detriment, on re-dubbing American actors with fake German accents in post-production. A sex scene between Law and Karen Huston was edited out after it caused an American preview audience to laugh.

It would be enticing to believe that the mutilation of *Gas-s-s-s!* and *Von Richthofen and Brown* by, respectively, AIP and United Artists served as the catalyst for Corman's decision to quit direction but, as Corman stated, 'No. I made that decision during shooting. The reviews were pretty good – as a matter of fact *The New York Times* listed it as one of the ten best pictures of the year that year. In America the reviews were pretty good.'

Story

Aristocratic (and autocratic) fighter pilot Baron Manfred von Richthofen is posted to an airfield in northern France where he is eventually given command of a squadron whose planes he orders to be painted in bright colours, earning them the nickname 'The Flying Circus'. He becomes 'The Red Baron' and German's most celebrated World War One air ace until, after some 80 kills to his credit, he is shot down and killed in 1918 by plebian Canadian Roy Brown who is serving with the Royal Air Force.

Corman underscores his central theme by giving Richthofen/Law the line 'My ancestors were Teutonic knights. I have merely exchanged the horse for a plane.' The production is large-scale and ambitious and as long as *Von Richthofen and Brown* is airborne, the action is thrilling and exhilarating. On the ground, however, the drama rarely takes off.

Reviews

'Dreary, ludicrous film based on actual World War I people and events. Needs hard sell, fast playoff. ... extremely dull, sometimes ludicrous ... After a slow but promising start, the Gene Corman production goes down in flames from a flat script compounded by wooden and flimsy performances ... Roger Corman's casual direction accomplishes the impossible – in that non-process aerial sequences and periodic dogfights leave an audience completely cold. The United Artists release needs a splashy saturation to overcome word of mouth ... storytelling is so bad that, in time, one begins to notice that single takes of supposedly damaged planes never show the crash; that strafing attacks create undue havoc (Peter Dawson's fine special effects are worthy of hydrogen bomb assault); and that phoney blood has been applied in buckets. Technical credits are professional, and Hugo Friedhofer's score helps the main titles.'
Variety

'Corman hasn't exactly chosen the easiest path for himself in making a film where not only the psychological conflicts, but the physical ones are interiorised. There are no dogfights conventionally staged for aerial excitement. Instead, stunning shots of the lazy, gaily painted biplanes and triplanes leave them hovering remote, detached from each other, until the appointed time comes for them to spiral to earth like Tennessee Williams' mythical wingless bird. Up there, one feels... men may be locked in combat, but it is down below that madness lies.'
Sight and Sound

'An extraordinarily impressive movie by a filmmaker whose career has not always been marked by success or even noble failure... in outline, *Von Richthofen and Brown* is a film of great simplicity... However, it is not the film's intention to reproduce history as much as it is to produce something more like a philosophical meditation on historical process, interpreted dramatically and interspersed with episodes of mortal combat. If you can take the idea of a philosophical meditation seriously, as I think this film, does, then something happens to the framework, to the magnificent aerial flights which are

important for their quality of almost disembodied freedom. They are very real in the sense that they capture the feeling of flight as a privileged way of being, rather than as a superheated adventure.'
The New York Times

CREDITS

Von Richtofen and Brown (US 1970)
(GB: **The Red Baron**)
pc The Corman Company **p** Gene Corman
assoc p, ad Jim C Murukami **d** Roger Corman
w John Corrington, Joyce Corrington **ph** Michael Reed
2nd unit ph Lynn Ellsworth, Neil Siegler
aerial ph Peter Allwork, Peter Pechowski, Seamus Corcoran
colour **ed** George van Noy, Alan Collins
sfx Peter Dawson **m** Hugo Friedhofer
97 mins
Cast: John Phillip Law (Baron Manfred von Richthofen), Don Stroud (Roy Brown), Barry Primus (Hermann Goering), Karen Huston (Ilse), Corin Redgrave (Lance Hawker), Hurd Hatfield (Fokker), Peter Masterson (Oswald Boelcke), Robert La Tourneaux (Udet), George Armitage (Wolff), Steve McHattie (Voss), Brian Foley (Lothar von Richtofen), David Osterhout (Holzapfel), Clint Kimbrough (Von Hoeppner), Gordon Phillips (Cargonico), Peadar Lamb (German Staff Major), Seamus Forde (Kaiser), Ferdy Mayne (Richtofen's Father), Maureen Cusack (Richtofen's Mother), Fred Johnson (Jeweller Funck), Vernon Hayden (Trackl), Michael Fahey (Richtofen aged 3), Robert Walsh (Richtofen aged 13), Tom Adams (Owen), David Weston (Murphy), Brian Sturdivant (May), Dos Nealon (British Intelligence Officer), John Flanagan (Thompson), Lorraine Rainier (Girl in the Woods)

FRANKENSTEIN UNBOUND

Corman stayed out of the director's chair for 20 years, during which time he produced around 140 movies for his New World and Concorde-New Horizon companies, confirmed their status as one of the last great independent studios and continued to advance the careers of some of America's brightest new filmmakers.

In 1990, he made a memorable return to direction with *Frankenstein Unbound*.

In the United States it was extremely well received and The New York Times *compared me to Fellini and Kurosawa.*
Roger Corman

Backstory

After Universal Pictures had conducted market research that showed a film with the title *Roger Corman's Frankenstein* would be a success, they approached Corman (who had been unaware of the research) to see if he would be interested in directing such a movie. He turned them down on the sensible basis that there were already some 50 or 60 *Frankenstein* films in existence.

He then passed on the project again when Universal made a second approach some 12 months later, since at that time he had no thoughts to bring to the subject that might make it a viable proposition and which would differentiate it from the large body of previous versions. However, when Universal's former head of production Robert Thom, who had now left the studio and was an independent producer, came to see Corman a year later, the project finally gelled.

'I remembered a novel called *Frankenstein Unbound* by Brian Aldiss that I'd read about 15 years earlier',

Corman told *Starburst*. 'I said if we could get that novel, which is a new way of looking at the *Frankenstein* story, I would be interested in doing that film.'

He wanted essentially to remain faithful to Aldiss but nevertheless made some specific changes which he incorporated into the first draft of the screenplay.

'One of the great traps in Hollywood is to buy a very good novel and then make so many changes that you lose the essence of the novel', he stated. 'We're totally faithful to the spirit of the novel, and in the sequences of the plotting, we're reasonably faithful, with a few additional ideas, but not many ... If there is a theme, it is the consequences that can occur from irresponsible scientific research.'

In order to underline this theme, he had the protagonist, Joe Buchanan, come from the future and changed him from the novel's retired diplomat to a scientist so that he would then be responsible for the Time Slip that transported him from the twenty-first century to the nineteenth and so learn that science is a two-edged sword 'which', says Corman, 'represents my personal belief'.

Corman succeeded in bringing off his two main concerns: he was able to propound an intelligent examination of the morality of scientific experimentation, while at the same time fulfilling the prime audience expectations of a horror/monster movie.

'I like the idea of horror by indirection rather than directly cutting off an arm and seeing the blood squirting across the screen,' he said. He also appreciated the more graphic violence and gore that was expected in contemporary genre pictures, although he noted 'I don't think of it specifically as horror. Effectively, it isn't pure

Frankenstein Unbound
1990 Corman returns: John Hurt plays Dr Joseph Buchanan and Nick Brimble is the monster

horror, it's more speculative science fiction.'

Corman told his leading actors, John Hurt and Raul Julia, that *Frankenstein Unbound* was, in the words of NBC television, 'A thinking man's horror film'. Hurt proved to be an ideal choice to play Buchanan who had to be both cerebral, passionate and not a little quirky, and Julia was equally aptly cast as Dr Frankenstein.

As Frankenstein's Creature, Nick Brimble had the daunting task of following in the footsteps of Boris Karloff and Christopher Lee.

Corman was determined to make his monster unique and not to hark back either to either of the classic creations from the James Whale and Terence Fisher *Frankenstein*s. With monster designer Nick Dudman he achieved the desired effect.

When Corman delivered the completed picture, it turned out to be shorter than his contract demanded and he was obliged to lengthen it.

However, he told *Starburst*, 'The picture is essentially the one I set out to make. I added maybe one or two minutes, and they were happy. It was kind of a compromise between the shorter, faster paced picture I wanted and the longer picture they wanted by contract.

'*Frankenstein Unbound* had good reviews in America,' Corman told me. 'To the best of my knowledge it never got a bad or even mediocre review. Every review ranged from good to excellent and it won a couple of film festivals. After a sneak preview I felt that a few things didn't play right, and I made some changes so that the changed version – which was improved in my opinion as a result of the sneak preview – was what was shown in the United States.

It did not get good reviews in England for reasons I don't totally understand. The English and foreign cut was a little bit different from the United States. The English cut was my original version – but I didn't make that many changes so I am somewhat puzzled. The reviews were so good in America – and the difference wasn't so great – I don't totally understand it.'

Corman remains philosophical about the differing receptions. 'Maybe the expectation was greater in England', he said, 'so if I didn't hit quite that level, they didn't like it. But maybe in America the expectation wasn't so high, so that when I did fairly good work they said, okay, this is all right.'

ory

2031, a scientist's experiments open a 'gate' in
ne that transports him and his computer-con-
olled car to Lake Geneva in 1813 where he
ncounters Dr Frankenstein, his rampaging
reature, Mary Shelley, Lord Byron and Percy
Byshe Shelley before he and the Creature are
hurled through time for a final confrontation in
an arid icebound future.

Corman serendipitously demonstrates that neither the
passage of time nor working with a large (for him) budget has diluted his skill as one of the prime purveyors of

genre movies. Those critics who complained *Corman's Frankenstein Unbound* was not Aldiss's *Frankenstein Unbound* were missing the point. There would have been little point in making a literal translation of the novel to the screen. Changes are inevitably required when a work is adapted from another medium to meet the parameters of film and Corman reworks the original in cinematic terms to considerable effect to create an intriguing piece that takes full advantage of the changes that had taken place in audience tastes and expectations since his last ventures into horror movies, while at the same time paying witty homage to his previous genre work. 'I don't think of it specifically as horror', he says. 'Effectively, it isn't pure horror; it's more speculative science fiction.'

Reviews

'Roger Corman's *Frankenstein Unbound* is a competent but uninspired riff on the venerable legend. Fans of the famous filmmaker will want to check out his first directorial debut since United Artists' *Von Richthofen and Brown* in 1971 ... film relies heavily on Hurt's modern car (a robot contraption à la tv's *Knight Rider*, with Concorde regular Terri Treas providing its female voice) ... though some of the dialogue is klutzy, acting is generally good ... Monster design by Nick Dudman is closer to Swamp Thing than the familiar '30s Karloff makeup, but is interesting ... there's enough gore to keep modern audiences contented. While lots of laser lights and optical effects keep things alive, Corman fails to keep the narrative advancing in riveting fashion. Hopefully he will continue to direct films and find his stride again.'
Variety

'... a strange and fanciful thing of snarls and patches. A head-on encounter with *Roger Corman's Frankenstein Unbound* is a bewildering experience, partly because we don't quite know what to expect after the 20-year hiatus, and partly because we are forced to realize that Corman doesn't either ... at his most authoritative, Corman directs with an appealing precision ... that the accents are all askew, that the inn, the trial, the execution, and the laboratory scenes are like clichés from the Hammer era, seems to bother him not at all. He films them with pace and an engaging sense of fun. That the 20-year respite may perhaps have coarsened him is suggested by the film's more violent details ... at his less confident, Corman's staging is

no better than functional.'
Monthly Film Bulletin

'You can't teach an old director new tricks and this wretched version of Brian Aldiss's *Frankenstein Unbound* proves it ... doggedly old-fashioned, you'd swear this was a Poe adaptation he never got around to making. Replace Hurt with Vincent Price, Nick *Batman* Dudman's *Swamp Thing* creature with a Paul Blaisdell monster, put the whole disaster in B&W and you'd be forgiven for mistaking this ludicrous passion play as one from his 50s heyday. Even the hopeless acting from all concerned fits the theory ... Bad it may be, yet it's an absolute must-see. Enormously entertaining for all the wrong reasons, there hasn't been a movie so refreshingly awful since, well, Corman's own *Gas-s-s-s!*'
Starburst

CREDITS 〉〉〉〉〉〉〉〉〉〉

Frankenstein Unbound/ Roger Corman's Frankenstein Unbound (US 1990)
pc Mount Co.
p Roger Corman, Thom Mount, Kabi Jaeger
assoc p Laura Medina, Jay Cassidy
d Roger Corman. 2nd unit d Thierry Notz
w Roger Corman, F X Feeny, (uncredited Ed Neumeir)
From the novel by Brian Aldiss
ph Armando Nannuzzi, Michael Scott
colour
ed Jay Cassidy, Mary Bauer
p design Enrico Tovaglieri
cost Franca Zuchelli
sfx/monster design Nick Dudman
sp visual fx Illusion Arts, Syd Dutton, Bill Taylor
add sp visual fx Gene Warren Jr.
m Carl Davis
stunt co-ordinator Paul Weston
85 mins
Cast: John Hurt (Dr John Buchanan), Raul Julia (Dr Frankenstein), Bridget Fonda (Mary Godwin), Nick Brimble (Frankenstein Monster), Catherine Rabett (Elizabeth), Jason Patric (Lord Byron), Michael Hutchence (Percy Shelley), Catherine Corman (Justine), Mickey Knox (General), Terri Treas (Voice of car)

CHILDREN

In 1996, Corman came to London to make his first film in England since *The Tomb of Ligeia* in 1964. It was to be his last movie as director to date.

Ironically, however, the commercial *Children* which he made for no payment for the environmental pressure group Greenpeace International, perversely turned out to be the only one of his films which had to be withdrawn because of the potential controversy it was believed its showing in cinemas and on satellite television would cause.

Other than give an occasional lecture at, say, the British Film Institute, this is the first time to the best of my knowledge that I have done something for nothing.
Roger Corman

Backstory

'When you've got zero budget and would like a great and experienced director, who better than Roger Corman?', stated Greenpeace International marketing director Daryl Upsall, adding: 'The degree of horror, *Lord of the Flies* imagery is perfect for Roger.'

The commercial, written by Paul Hodgkinson, shows a naked Mother Earth being cuddled, then beaten and finally stabbed to death by a group of naked children. Inevitably the British media made much of the fact that Greenpeace had engaged the director of such films as *The Pit and The Pendulum, Swamp Woman* and *Bucket of Blood* and also (said *The Guardian*) 'the man who brought us the likes of *Teenage Doll, Death Race 2000, Bloody Mama* and *Big Bad Mama*' to make it.

Greenpeace and their advertising agency justified the nudity by saying it would prevent audiences from being able to identify a specific nationality or a particular location, and Greenpeace wrote in a letter to the parents of the children who took part in the film, 'You should be assured that our film will be shot with every care for

the dignity of the cast, and will in no way exploit the innocence of its members ... There is a simple reason why we are shooting this way, and we believe that our message is powerful enough to override petty hang-ups. We are also certain that our sensitive treatment of nudity will expose negative criticism as foolish and gratuitous.'

In the event, however, that certainty proved to be unfounded.

'It strikes me as very strange', Corman commented. 'For instance, the concept that Mother Earth should be nude was one of the ideas we were working with. I remember speaking to the people, the producer and the staff, and I said, she could be nude or she could have some sort of an earth-like clinging costume, or we could do what I did with *The Trip* where I used body paint, and paint her in some way.

'I said, there are so many good painters in England who would like to work with Greenpeace. They might be able to give us something really wonderful, either as body paint or a body glove over it. But it was finally decided to do it nude, and I said fine. But I felt there might be a problem but they said, "No, No. There'll be no problem here." And then the problem arose. And the problem evidently was *not* so much the fact that our Mother Earth was nude – it was the fact that there were children around our Mother Earth and *they* were also nude. And that is evidently what brought the censorship. There had been stories of child abuse in England and they were worried about that. I think when the commercial was conceived they were not worried about it. But after I shot it, these things happened and they were in the headlines and people then started to become very worried about this and somebody on some level censored it.'

When the film was withdrawn, *The Observer* ran the headline 'Paedophile fears kill Greenpeace ad' over the story and quoted Greenpeace UK marketing director Annie Morton as saying, 'Child abuse is an issue in this country and for this reason I would not run it,' while, said advertising agency writer Paul Hodgkinson, 'If people are concerned about naked children, then it's all in their minds. The ad's overriding message points out the importance of saving the world from disaster.'

An appropriate message, perhaps, for the director who had already overseen the end of the world over 40 years previously in *The Day the World Ended*.

Director filmography

*Beast with a Million Eyes/Beast with
1,000,000 Eyes* (1955) (uncredited)
Five Guns West (1954)
The Oklahoma Woman (1955)
Apache Woman (1955)
Swamp Woman (1955)
The Day the World Ended (1955)
Gunslinger (1956)
It Conquered the World/It Conquered the Earth
(1956)
Attack of the Crab Monsters (1957)
Not of this Earth (1957)
Naked Paradise/Thunder Over Hawaii (1957)
Teenage Doll (1957)
Carnival Rock (1957)
Rock all Night (1957)
*Sage of the Viking Women and Their Voyage to
the Waters of the Great Sea Serpent,
The/Viking Women and the Sea Serpent,
The/ Saga of the Viking/Undersea Monster/*
(GB: *Viking Women*) (1957)
Sorority Girl (GB: *The Bad One*) (1957)
She-Gods of Shark Reef (GB: *Shark Reef*)
(1957)
Attack of the Crab Monsters (1957)
I, Mobster (GB: *The Mobster*) (1958)
Machine Gun Kelly (1958)
War of the Satellites (1958)
Last Woman on Earth, The (1958)
Teenage Caveman/Prehistoric World (GB: *Out
of the Dark*) (1958)
A Bucket of Blood (1959)
Wasp Woman, The (1959)
Little Shop of Horrors, The (1960)
Atlas (1960)
Creature from the Haunted Sea (1960)
Ski Troop Attack (1960)
House of Usher (GB: *The Fall of the House of
Usher*) (1960)
The Intruder/I Hate Your Guts! (GB: *The
Stranger*) (1961)
The Pit and the Pendulum (1961)
Poe's Tales of Terror (GB: *Tales of Terror*) (1962)
The Premature Burial (1962)
Tower of London (1962)
The Young Racers (1963)
*X-The Man With the X-Ray Eyes/Man with
the X-Ray Eyes/X* (1963)
The Raven (1963)
The Terror (1963)
The Haunted Palace (1963)
The Masque of the Red Death (1964)
The Tomb of Ligeia (1964)
The Secret Invasion (1964)
The Wild Angels (1966)
A Time For Killing
(1966 - part d, uncredited)

The Trip (1967)
The St Valentine's Day Massacre (67)
De Sade (1969 - part d, unaccredited)
How to Make it (GB: *Target Harry*) (TVM
1969)
Bloody Mama (1969)
*Gas-s-s- or: It Became Necessary to Destroy
the World in Order to Save it* (1970)
Von Richthofen and Brown (GB: *The Red
Baron*) (1971)
*Frankenstein Unbound/Roger Corman's
Frankenstein Unbound* (1990)
Children (1996)

Producer filmography

Highway Dragnet (1955)
(co-produced, co-w)
*Monster From the Ocean Floor/It Stalked the
Ocean Floor/Monster Maker* (1954)
Fast and the Furious, The (1954)
Five Guns West (1955)
Oklahoma Woman, The (1956)
It Conquered the World (1956)
Gunslinger, The (1956)
Hot Rod Girl/Hot Car Girl (1956) (execu-
tive)
Day the World Ended, The (1956)
Beast With 1,000 Eyes (1956) (executive)
Teenage Doll (1957)
Sorority Girl (1957)
Rock all Night (1957)
Not of this Earth (1957)
Naked Paradise/Thunder Over Hawaii (1957)
Carnival Rock (1957)
Attack of the Crab Monsters (1957)
War of the Satellites (1958)
*Teenage Caveman/Out of the
Darkness/Prehistoric World* (1958)
*Saga of the Viking Women and their Voyage to
the Waters of the Great Sea Serpent/Saga of
the Viking, The/Undersea Monster/Viking
Women/Viking Women and the Sea Serpent*
(1958)
*Night of the Blood Beast/Creature from
Galaxy 27/Monster from Galaxy 27*
(1958) (executive)
Machine Gun Kelly (1958)
Cry Baby Killer (1958)
Brain Eaters, The (1958) (executive)
Stakeout on Dope Street (1958) (executive)
T-Bird Gang/The Pay-Off (1958)
High School Big Shot (1959) (executive)
Bucket of Blood, A (1959)
Crime and Punishment USA (1959)
(executive)
Beast From Haunted Cave (1959) (executive)

Wasp Woman, The (1960)
Battle of Blood Island (1960)

Little Shop of Horrors, The (1960)
Last Woman on Earth, The (1960)
House of Usher/Fall of the House of Usher
(1960)
*Attack of the Giant Leeches/Attack of the
Blood Leeches/Demons of the Swamp/Giant
Leeches, The* (1960) (executive)
Atlas (1960)
Wild Ride, The (1961)
Pit and the Pendulum, The (1961)
Creature from the Haunted Sea (1961)
Tales of Terror (1962)
Premature Burial, The (1962)
*X - the Man With the X-Ray Eyes/Man With
the X-Ray Eyes/X* (1963)
Terror, The (1963)
Raven, The (1963)
Pit Stop (1963)
Haunted Palace (1963)
Moving Violation (1963)
Young Racers, The (1963)
Magic Voyage of Sinbad (1963)
Battle Beyond the Sun (1963)
(Nebo Zovyot 1959)
Dementia 13/The Haunted and the Hunted
(1963)
Masque of the Red Death (1964)
*Voyage to the Prehistoric Planet/Prehistoric
Planet/Voyage to a Prehistoric Planet* (1965)
(executive)
Beach Ball (1965)
Queen of Blood (1965)
Ride the Whirlwind (1965) (uncredited)
Wild Angels, The (1966)
*Queen of Blood/Flight to the Far Planet/Green
Woman, The/Planet of Blood/Planet of
Vampires* (1966) (executive)
Blood Bath (1966) (executive)
Trip, The (1967)
Devil's Angels (1967)
Time for Killing, A (1967) (co-producer)
(uncredited direction of some scenes)
*Voyage to the Planet of Prehistoric Women/Gill
Women of Venus, The/ Gill Women, The*
(1968)
Targets (executive) (1968)
Wild Racers, The (1968)

---

*Ivanna/Blood Castle/Il Castello dalle porte del
fuoco/Killers of the Castle of Blood/Scream
of the Demon Lover* (1970/1)
*Gass-s-s/Gas! Or It Became Necessary to
Destroy the World in Order to Save It/Gas-
s-s-s ... or, it May Become Necessary to
Destroy the World in Order to Save It*
(1970)
Dunwich Horror, The (1970) (executive)
Student Nurses, The (1970)
Bloody Mama (1970)

Women in Cages/Women's Penitentiary III (1971)

Private Duty Nurses (1971) (executive)

Angels Die Hard! (1971)

Big Doll House/Bamboo Dolls House/Women's Penitentiary/Woman's Penitentiary (1971)

Women in Cages (1971)

Unholy Rollers/Leader of the Pack (1972) (executive)

Twilight People/Beasts (1972) (executive)

Hot Box, The (1972) (executive)

Cremators, the/Dune Rollers (1972)

Twilight People, The/Beasts/Island of the Twilight People (1972) (executive)

Lady Frankenstein (1972)

Night of the Cobra Woman/Movini's Venom (1972)

Sweet Kill (1972)

Angels, Hard as They Come (1972)

Night Call Nurses (1972)

The Final Comedown/Blast (1972)

Boxcar Bertha (1972)

Private Duty Nurses (1972)

Bury Me an Angel (1972)

Big Bird Cage, The (1972)

I Escaped From Devil's Island (1973)

Arena, The (1973)

Savage! (1973)

Young Nurses, The (1973)

Student Teachers, The (1973)

Fly Me (1973)

Candy Stripe Nurses (1974)

Tender Loving Care (1974)

Cockfighters/Born to Kill/Gamblin' Man/Wild Drifter (1974)

Caged Heat/Caged Females/Renegade Girls (1974)

Big Bad Mama (1974)

Grotesque (1975)

Death Race 2000 (1975)

Capone (1975)

Moving Violation (1975)

Crazy Mama (1975)

Tidal Wave (1975)

Fighting Mad (1975)

Cover Girl Models (1975)

Jackson County Jail (1976) (executive)

Fighting Mad (1976)

Summer School Teachers (1976)

Hollywood Boulevard (1976)

Cannonball (1976)

Eat My Dust! (1976)

Grand Theft Auto (1977) (executive)

Great Texas Dynamite Chase, The (1977)

I Never Promised You a Rose Garden (co-executive)

Thunder and Lightning/Thunder on the Highway (1977)

Tigress/Ilsa, the Tigress of Siberia (1978)

Avalanche (1978)

Deathsport (1978)

Piranha (1978) (co-executive)

Outside Chance/Return to Jackson County Jail (TVM, 1978) (co-produced)

Up From the Depths (1979) (executive)

Saint Jack (1979)

Rock 'n' Roll High School (1979) (executive)

Fast Charlie, The Moonbeam Rider/Fast Charlie and the Moonbeam (1979)

Humanoids from the Deep/Humanoids of the Deep/Monster/Monsters (1980)

Galaxy Express 999/Galaxy Express/Galaxy Express 999: Can You Like Like a Warrior?/Galaxy Express 999: Can You Love Like a Mother (1980) (executive)

Battle Beyond the Stars (1980)

Territory, The/Le Territoire (1981)

Smokey Bites the Dust (1981)

Galaxy of Terror/Mindwarp: An Infinity of Terror/Planet of Horrors/ Quest (1981)

Saturday the 14th (1981)

Warrior and the Sorceress, The/Kain of the Dark Planet/Kain Del Planet Oscuro (1982)

Forbidden World/Mutant (1982)

State of Things, The/Der Stande Der Dinge (1983)

Wild Side, The/Suburbia (1983)

Love Letters/My Love Letters (1983)

Space Raiders/Star Child (1983)

Hell's Angels Forever (1983)

Oddballs (1984) (executive)

Deathstalker (1984)

Sorority House Massacre (1986) (executive) (uncredited)

Cocaine Wars/Vice Wars (1986) (co-produced)

Stripped To Kill/Deception (1987)

Munchies (1987)

Sweet Revenge (1987)

Summer Camp Nightmare/The Butterfly Revolution (1987) (executive)

Hour of the Assassin (1987) (executive)

Big Bad Mama II (1987)

Daddy's Boys (1987)

Lawless Land, The (1988) (co-executive)

Drifter, The (1988) (executive)

Crime Zone (1988) (executive)

New Gladiators, The (1988) (executive)

Matares, orir un poco/Two To Tango (1988) (co-producer)

Blackbelt II/Blackbelt II: Fatal Force/Spyder (1988) (executive)

Andy Colby's Incredible Adventure/Andy Colby's Incredible Video Adventure/Andy Colby's Incredibly Awesome Adventure/Andy and the Airwave Rangers (1988) (executive)

Emmanuelle VI (1988) (executive)

Silk 2 (1989) (executive)

Watchers (1988)

Dance of the Damned/Half Life (1988)

Masque of the Red Death (1989)

Primary Target (1989) (executive)

Heroes Stand Alone (1989) (executive)

Transylvania Twist (1989) (executive)

Heroes Stand Alone (1989) (executive)

Bloodfist (1989)

Time Trackers (1989)

Terror Within, The (1989)

Terror Within II, The (1990) (executive)

Overexposed (1990)

Last Stand at Lang Mei/Eye of the Eagle 3 (1990)

Haunting of Morella, The (1990)

Full Fathom Five (1990)

Frankenstein Unbound/Roger Corman's Frankenstein Unbound (1990)

Dune Warriors (1990)

Deathstalker IV: Match of the Titans/Deathstalker IV/Deathstalker IV: The Darkest Hour (1990) (executive)

Bloodfist II (1990)

Back to Back (1990)

Play Murder for Me (1990)

Streets (1990)

Killer Instinct/Homicidal Impulse (1991)

Field of Fire (1991)

Cry in the Wild, A (1991)

Hollywood Boulevard II (1991)

Futurekick (1991)

Besos en la oscuridad (1991)/*US: Immortal Sins* (1992)

Ultraviolet (1992) (executive)

Welcome to Oblivion (1992)

Sorority House Massacre 2 (1992)

Play Murder for Me (1992)

Raiders of the Sun (1992)

Body Chemistry II: The Voice of a Stranger/Voice of a Stranger (1992) (executive)

Homicidal Impulse (1992)

Field of Fire (1992)

Eye of the Eagle 3 (1992)

Deathstalker IV: Match of Titans (1992)

Dance With Death (1992)

Body Waves (1992)

Bloodfist III: Forced to Fight (1992)

Bloodfist IV: Die Trying (1992)

Blackbelt (1992) (executive)

Beyond the Call of Duty (1992)

Live by the Fist (1993)

Skateboard Kid, The (1993) (executive)

To Sleep With a Vampire (1993)

Little Miss Millions/Home for Christmas (1993)

Stepmonster (1993)
Live By the Fist (1993)
Kill Zone (1993)
Firehawk (1993)
Emmanuelle VI (1993) (executive)
Dragon Fire (1993) (executive)
Dracula Rising (1993)
Carnosaur (1993) (executive)
Angelfist (1993)
Assassination Game, The (1993)
800 Leagues Down the Amazon (1993)
Watchers III (1993)
In the Heat of Passion II: Unfaithful/Unfaithful (1994)
Unborn II, The (1994)
Little Miss Millions (1994)
Stranglehold (1994) (executive)
Reflections on a Crime/Reflections in the Dark (1994) (executive)
One Man Army/Kick & Fury (1994)
No Dessert Dad, Til You Mow the Lawn (1994) (executive)
New Crime City (1994) (executive)
Flight of the Dove/The Spy Within (1994) (executive)
Deadly Desire/Saturday Night Special (1994) (executive)
Cheyenne Warrior (TVM, 1994) (executive)
Final Embrace (1994)
Fantastic Four, The (1994) (executive)
Caroline at Midnight (1994)
Bloodfist VI: Ground Zero/Assault at Ground Zero/Ground Zero (1994) (executive)
Bucket of Blood/Dark Secrets/Death Artist, The/Roger Corman Presents Bucket of Blood (TVM, 1995) (executive)
Angel of Destruction/Furious Angel (1994) (executive)
Dillinger and Capone (1995) (executive)
Droid Gunner/Cyberzone (1995) (executive)
Where Evil Lies (1995) (executive)
Terminal Virus (TVM, 1995) (executive)
Piranha/Roger Corman Presents Piranha (TVM, 1995) (executive)
Unknown Origin/The Alien Within (TVM, 1995) (executive)
Wasp Woman, The/aka Forbidden Beauty/Roger Corman Presents The Wasp Woman (TVM, 1995)
Twisted Love (1995) (executive)
Suspect Device/Roger Corman Presents Suspect Device (TVM, 1995) (executive)
One Night Stand/Before the Night (1995) (executive)
Not of this Earth (1995) (executive)
Last Chance (1995) (executive)
Hellfire/Blood Song/Haunted Symphony/Roger Corman Presents Hellfire (TVM, 1995) (executive)

Crazysitter, The (1995) (executive)
Captain Nuke and the Bomber Boys/Demolition Day (1995) (executive)
Caged Heat 3000 (1995) (executive)
Burial of the Rats/Bram Stoker's 'Burial of the Rats'/Roger Corman Presents Burial of the Rats (TVM, 1995) (executive)
Bloodfist VII/Manhunt (1995) (executive)
Black Rose of Harlem/Machine Gun Blues/Pistol Blues (1995) (executive)
Baby Face Nelson (1995) (executive)
Black Scorpion/Roger Corman Presents Black Scorpion (TVM, 1995) (executive)
Vampirella (1996) (executive)
Unspeakable, The/Roger Corman Presents The Unspeakable (TVM, 1996) (executive)
Subliminal Seduction/Roger Corman Presents Subliminal Seduction (TVM, 1996) (executive)
Humanoids from the Deep/Roger Corman Presents Humanoids from the Deep (TVM, 1996) (executive)
Last Exit to Earth/Roger Corman Presents Last Exit to Earth (TVM, 1996) (executive)
Death Game (TVM 1996) (executive)
Carnosaur 3: Primal Species (1996)
Black Scorpion II: Aftershock (1996) (executive)
Alien Avengers/Roger Corman Presents Alien Avengers/Welcome to Planet Earth (TVM, 1997) (executive)
Born Bad (1997) (executive)
Circuit Breaker (1997) (executive)
Club Vampire (1997) (executive)
Crossroads of Destiny/Macon County Jail (1997) (executive)
Detonator (1997) (executive)
Don't Sleep Alone (1997) (executive)
Eruption (1997) (executive)
Falling Fire (1997) (executive)
Haunted Sea/Ghost Ship (1997) (executive)
Overdrive (1997) (executive)
Physical Attraction (1997) (executive)
Sea Wolf, The/Jack London's The Sea Wolf (1997) (executive)
Starquest II/Mind Breakers (1997) (executive)
Striptease II (1997) (executive)
Urban Justice/Blood Money/Under Oath (1997) (executive)
Vatican Air Two (1998)

Writer filmography
Fast and the Furious (1954) (story)
Terror, The (1963)
Frankenstein Unbound/Roger Corman's Frankenstein Unbound (1990)

Actor filmography
War of the Satellites (1958) Ground Controller
Cry Baby Killer, The (1958) (uncredited)
Ski Troop Attack (1960) (uncredited)
Creature from the Haunted Sea (1960)
Godfather: Part II, The (1974) Senator #2
Cannonball/Carquake (1976)
Howling, The (1981) Man in phone booth: uncredited
Stand der Dinge, Der/Estado das coisas, O/State of Things, The (1982 – The Lawyer)
Swing Shift (1984) Mr MacBride
Lords of the Deep (1989)
Hollywood Boulevard II (1989)
Silence of the Lambs, The (1991) FBI Director Hayden Burke
Philadelphia (1993) Mr Laird
Body Bags/John Carpenter Presents Body Bags (TVM 1993) Dr Bregman
Century of Cinema, A (1994)
Runaway Daughters (TVM 1994) Mr Randolph
Apollo 13 (1995) Congressman
Second Civil War, The (TVM, 1997) Sandy Collins

Bibliography
Castle of Frankenstein, CEA Film Report
Cinefantastique, Cinefex, CinemaTV Today
Cult Films, Daily Express, Daily Mail
Daily Variety, The Dark Side, Empire, Famous Monsters of Filmland, Fandom's Film Galley
Fangoria, Fantastic Films, Film Bulletin, Film Collector, Film Monthly, Filmfax, Films in Review, Films Illustrated, Focus on Film
Hollywood Reporter, The Horror Elite, The Independent, The Independent on Sunday
Kinematograph Weekly, L'Ecran Fantastique
Little Shop of Horrors, The Los Angeles Times
Midi Minuit Fantastique, Midnight Marquee
Monthly Film Bulletin, Motion Picture Herald
Motion Picture Renter, Movie Collector's World
New York, The New York Times, The Observer
Photon, Photoplay, Picturegoer, Picture Show
Premiere, Radio Times, Screen International
Starburst, Starlog, The Sunday Times
Time Out, The Times, Today's Cinema
TV Guide, The Z-Z of Science Fiction and Fantasy FIlms: Howard Maxford (B T Batsford 1997)
American Film: James Monaco (Plume/New American Library 1979)
The Aurum Film Encyclopedia Horror: ed Phil Hardy (Aurum Press 1993)
The Aurum Film Encyclopedia Science Fiction: ed Phil Hardy (Aurum Press 1991)
The Aurum Film Encylopedia The Western: ed Phil Hardy (Aurum Press 1995)
Basil Rathbone, His Life and his Films: Michael B Druxman (Doubleday 1973)
The Big Book of B Movies or How Low Was My Budget: Robin Cross (Muller 1981)

Caligari's Children: S S Prawer (Oxford University Press 1980)

Les Classiques du Cinéma Fantastique: JeanMarie Sabatier (Editions Balland 1973)

Creature Features: John Stanley (Boulevard/Berkley 1997)

Crime Movies An Illustrated History: Carlos Clarens (Secker and Warburg 1980)

The Critics' Film Guide: Christopher Tookey (Boxtree 1994)

Cult Flicks and Trash Pics (Visible Ink Press 1996)

Cult Movies: Danny Peary (Vermilion 1981)

Cult Movies 2: Danny Peary (Vermiliom 1984)

Cult Movies 3: Danny Peary (Fireside Books/Sidgwick and Jackson 1988)

Faster and Furiouser: Mark Thomas McGee (McFarland 1996)

The Films of Roger Corman: Brilliance on a Budget: Ed Naha (Arco 1982)

Flying Through Hollywood By the Seat of my Pants: Sam Arkoff with Richard Trubo (Birch Lane Press/Carol 1992)

For One Week Only The World of Exploitation Films: Richard Meyers (New Century Publishers 1983)

The Great Science Fiction Pictures: James Robert Parrish and Michael R Pitts (Scarecrow Press 1997)

Guide for the Film Fanatic: Danny Peary (Simon and Schuster 1987)

A Heritage of Horror: David Pirie (Avon 1974)

Heroes of the Horrors: Calvin T Beck (Collier 1975)

Hoffman's Guide to SF, Horror and Fantasy Movies 1991-92 (Corgi 1991)

Horror A Connoisseur's Guide to Literature and Film: Leonard Wolf (Facts on File 1989)

Horror and Science Fiction Films: Donald C Willis (The Scarecrow Press 1972)

Horror and Science Fiction Films II: Donald C Willis (The Scarecrow Press 1982)

Horror and Science Fiction Films III: Donald C Willis (The Scarecrow Press 1984)

Horror Film Album: Alan Eyles (Ian Allen 1971)

The Horror Film Handbook: Alan Frank (B T Batsford 1980)

Horror in the Cinema: Ivan Butler (Zwemmer Barnes 1970)

Horror Movies: An Illustrated Survey: Carlos Clarens (Secker and Warburg)

The Horror People: John Brosnan (Macdonald and Janes 1974)

How I Made a Hundred Movies in Hollywood and Never Lost a Dime: Roger Corman with Jim Jerome (Muller 1990)

The I Was a Teenage Juvenile Delinquent Rock 'N' Roll Horror Beach Party Movie Book: Alan Betrock (St Martin's Press 1986)

The Illustrated Guide to Film Directors: David Quinlan (B T Batsford 1983)

The International Film Index 1895/1990: Volumes 1 & 2: ed Alan Goble (Bowker-Sauer 1991)

Interviews with B Science Fiction and Horror Movie Makers: Tom Weaver (McFarland 1988)

Boris Karloff and his Films: Paul M Jensen (Barnes 1974)

Keep Watching the Skies!: Bill Warren (McFarland 1982)

Keep Watching the Skies! Volume II: Bill Warren (McFarland 1986)

Kings of the Bs Working Within the Hollywood System: Ed Todd McCarthy and *Motion Picture Guide* (Cinebooks)

The Movie World of Roger Corman: ed Philip Di Franco (Chelsea House 1979)

Musique Fantastique: Randall D Larson (The Scarecrow Press 1985)

The Primal Scream: John Brosnan (Orbit 1991)

The Psychotronic Video Guide: Michael J Warren (St Martin's Press 1995)

Quinlan's Film Character Actors: David Quinlan (B T Batsford 1995)

Quinlan's Film Stars: David Quinlan (B T Batsford 1996)

Reference Guide to Fantastic Film (Three volumes): Walt Lee (Chelsea-Lee Books 1972, 1973, 1974)

Roger Corman: a cura di Emanuela Martini (Bergamo Film Meeting '91)

Roger Corman: The Best of the Cheap Acts: Mark Thomas McGee (McFarland 1988)

Roger Corman: The Millenic Vision: Paul Willemen, David Pirie, David Will, Lynda Mules (Edinburgh Film Festival 70/Cinema Magazine)

The Science Fiction and Fantasy Film Handbook: Alan Frank (B T Batsford 1982)

Science Fiction, Horror and Fantasy Film and TV Credits: Harris M Lentz III (McFarland 1983)

Le Science Fiction au Cinéma: Jean-Pierre Bouyxou (Union Général D'Editions 1971)

Science Fiction in the Cinema: John Baxter (Zwemmer Barnes 1970)

The Science Fictionary: Ed Naha (Wideview Books 1980)

Sleaze Creatures: D Earl Worth (Fantasma Books 1995)

Slimetime: Steven Puchalski (Headpress 1996)

Time Out Film Guide 5: ed John Pym (Penguin 1996)

ViedeoHound's Golden Movie Retriever 1998: ed Martin Connors & Jim Craddock (Visible Ink Press 1998) www.imdp.com

Western Movies: Michael R Pitts (McFarland 1986)

Stills are copyright of the production companies as credited

Abbreviations

ad	art director
assoc p	associate producer
bw	black and white
cost	costumes
d	director
ed	editor
m	music
mu	makeup
p	producer
pc	production company
p design	production design
ph	photography
sfx	special effects
sp ph fx	special photographic effects
st	story
w	screenwriter

Index